ANCHOR POETS

FROM THE

NORTH WEST

Foreword

Anchor Books is a small press, established in 1992, with the aim of promoting readable poetry to as wide an audience as possible.

The poems in *Anchor Poets From The North West* represent a cross-section of style and content.

These poems are written by young and old alike, united in their passion for writing poetry.

I trust this selection will delight and please the authors from *The North West* and all those who enjoy reading poetry.

Andrew Head
Editor

CONTENTS

BACK IN SUBURBIA

Down at the station
The commuters await,
The next train to the city
The eight thirty eight.

The noise and commotion
Crashes and dins,
The commuters destination
The city of sins.

Meanwhile back in Suburbia
All is quiet and serene.
These streets far removed
From the city machine.

No hustle and bustle,
Just life passing by.
Peace and tranquillity,
A vision to espy.

But this perfect ideal
Is not all what it may seem.
For the commuters will return
And shatter this dream.

Then back in the city
All will be quiet and serene.
Now devoid of life
Like the daily Suburban machine.

Andrew Pennington

LIVERPOOL

The river Mersey is cold and drear
On a winter day it's without much cheer.
Folk talk of this city and football many a time
And of how on that game men will spend their last dime.
It's true we have Anfield and Everton
A new manager and possibly a new striker won.

But there's more to this city than meets the eye
Just take a walk and as you pass by
View the buildings and gargoyles in Castle Street
Who knows that by chance a Diddy man you might meet,
Having a day off from the Jam Butty Mines
So just doff your hat and smile and don't whine
About the wind and the weather on a cold winter's day
And ask him to come with you as you go on your way.

Go down to the Pier Head and see the Liver Buildings too
Look over to New Brighton and admire the view.
For Diddy Men originate from Knotty Ash
And that's where Ken Dodd lives with all his cash!
Tell him about the Beatles and show him Penny Lane
For a Diddy Man might not know of their sixties fame.
Take him up to the Cathedrals and around the town,
He's sure to like Rodney Street and Clayton Square as you bring him down.

There's so much more to Liverpool than first meets the eye
So just don't let visitors rush hurriedly by
Let us show off this city with pride not regret
And make it a place they don't want to forget.

Clare Owens

MY CITY

A simple word, a name
And yet it conjures up so many images -
Riots, unemployment, violence and hatred.
Why do these always come to the fore?
What about the marvels this city has to offer?
The sheer beauty of its architecture,
The tranquillity of a ferry ride across the River Mersey,
The all consuming good nature of its fellow men.
Yes, we have our share of bad too,
But so does every city nowadays.
Compensation is however provided -
By the unending glint of the Liver Birds' wings;
The gaze of Minerva over her people,
The unforgotten ballads of the Beatles,
As Eleanor Rigby still sits and Penny Lane remains.
The wave of football scarves - blue and red,
A constant reminder of football fame.
Yes, this is the city where riots took place, where unemployment was rife;
But also where united we stand, both in grief and joy.
And if you were to walk through one of our daffodil laden *fields of hope*,
Or gaze out across our maritime port,
Would you associate only trouble and strife,
With this bustling, energetic oasis?
This watering hole in the desert, where unlimited refreshment can be found.
If you were to experience the humour of its inhabitants,
Or walk through the crowded streets and hear the shouts of *Echo, Echo,*
Or taste a plate of scouse,
You would realise that this is a city where the spirit will never die,
And like me returning to its shores once again, you would realise -
This is Liverpool, this is home.

Joy Owens

SOUTHPORT BEACH

Sunglasses - for the glare;
Golden orb beats; a perfect sound.
Boys, girls dash 'cross the hills,
Feet swallowed, go to ground -
Sand seems to hide a secret -
Which never must be found.
Football, cricket, golf, and more,
Daydreams in the sun;
Sport heroes; so it's either: goal,
Hit six, or hole-in-one.
Mums and Dads, in deckchairs lie;
One burns - the other browns.
While children swim and splash,
Red flags alert - so no one drowns.
A driver wanders way too far;
Wheels sink; he needs a tow -
A rescue team; his car to save;
To keep it from the flow.
Jellyfish, like tiny pools,
Wait silent, in the heat,
Still sharp - their sting, for soft, bare skin -
That comes with careless feet.
The *shrimpers* scour the lonely paths,
To gather up *the feast* -
Whose fate - shelled, when boiled, then it's butter baths -
Ends in *luxury*, at least.
The crowds repair their ways ahead,
As daylight softly goes,
Relaxed, but know, there's nothing worse
Than sand - between your toes.

Andrew Clough

THE GRAVEYARD

A creaking gate, with rusted latch and oil-less hinge
Gapes open; the infirm guardian of a decaying world.
Cold granite slabs, grim monoliths of stone
In silhouette against a darkening sky,
Like moss encrusted fingers, scarred by time.
Reminders of departed souls, in ragged ranks arranged,
Their symmetry awry.
Pointing ever skyward, in silent stony protest
Against the fates who delegate such weary tasks.

Hear whispers of a sighing wind, searching ever searching
Through dripping fern, down shaded paths,
Seeking - who can tell, for life perhaps.
Some hint that in the wilderness a spark remains,
Though knotted boughs from long neglected shrubs
Arch and twine across each secret plot,
As though to grasp in some obscene embrace,
The lifeless forms interred beneath the mound.

Sun's feeble rays attempt to pierce the sullen gloom,
But barred by monstrous elm and sycamore, the fitful glow
Can scarce erase the stain. Leaving each dark corner
A remnant of some dismal night when chaos ruled.

Yet perched upon the withered branch, a blackbird,
Puffed out with self-importance like a town-hall clerk,
Invades this modern Hades with his trill.
And a girl with golden hair cries out in childish glee.
She leads me gently by the hand and points
To where the bluebells are massed upon the bank.
The nest she found, the squirrels' drey and other mysteries.
So I am shown, by youthful innocence,
An ancient yet unalterable law. Life Rules! OK.

Derek J Rogerson

ON THE RAZZ

Me Dad's gorra gob on cos I was off out;
he thinks I'll meet up with a divvy,
but I like the type who'll have a good crack,
without being too silly.

I'd done me hair up really nice,
blonde but carefully messy.
Put on me best dress, not *too* tight
and some white shoes I had for a pressic.

I was careful with me lip gloss, liberal with the talc
(you never know who's passin)
Eau de L'amour dabbed just enough
(I want to seduce - not gas him)

Pleased and excited, I thought I looked great
and added the finishing touch.
A long pendant necklace and dangly earrings
that didn't cost too much.

The music was pumping, the party full on
when I spotted *the lucky fella.*
Quite tasty and hunky (through lager top eyes)
shame his jacket was violent yella.

I thought I'd copped off, I was so full of charm;
and opened me gob for a smacker
he liked me for me personality and wit
and said I was a cracker.

His mates started laffin and he started to yell.
What a flamin racket!
Just cos me stiletto had caught on his foot
and me lipstick smudged on his jacket.

He should worry! Me best jewels were broken
(They'd snagged on his pointy collar)
Shame - cos we hadn't even spoken
Still, in for a penny in for a dollar?

Well I had a good time though me head's a bit sore
(I'd been ill in the back of the taxi)
I'll have a night in and fix me ripped dress
and look forward to watching *Brookie!*

Ellis O'Brien

AVALON VISITED

Avalon set as a diamond in a sea of emerald
Rising from the depths of green and blue
To stand with majesty, towering over the mundane worlds.
The land showered with every shade of green,
The browns of heather mingle under the yellows of gorse.

Glens, deep and gentle, drifting waves of scented air,
Glades of filtered sunlight shimmering with life,
Trees giving shade and shelter to the traveller.
Wild garlic, freshly cut grass, bees transfer pollen
Creating new growth.

Air tinged with salt, to cleanse and refresh,
Clouds sail over as horses gallop by,
Running for pleasure, to feel at full pelt,
Aching with life to explode with the joy.

Avalon, the soul's long search over,
Created by gods for all men to live for,
Always may there be a place in my heart,
Where we may reside in quiet communion.

Your magic and mystery
Long may they reign
Untarnished by blight
Or man's sad refrain.

P R C Colville

METEORIC RISE

A complex web of intricacies,
Behold the yielding sword,
Fear not the mortal coil,
For it awaits release from the depths.
Arising like a Phoenix from the ashes,
To calm awhile until explosions
Beyond anyone's dreams exist.
Dramatic rhetoric is the only option
Open to such description.
Fail not for destiny is in the stars.
Even the universe cannot emulate
The vast proportions of this meteoric rise.

Vikki Harker

TICK TOC

Tick toc, tick toc,
The sound of the calming clock,
Goes through my mind,
Like a mystic find,
Like a branch on a tree,
Branching out in me,
Tick then toc,
Goes the calming clock,
Like a flower on a stalk,
Forking out like a fork,
Like a constant drum,
Like a bee's sweet hum,
Tick toc, tick toc,
The sound of the calming clock.

Amy Monroe

LOUVRE METRO

Reflections of Egypt haunt the cavernous tomb
Counterfeit art neath Europe's cultural womb
Originals baggage for Pharaoh's ascendance
Copies adornment for Louvre Metro's resplendence

No clattering contraption; nor cast iron relic
No howling banshee; nor transport angelic
Mere soft seated comfort, swift, silent and smooth
Moves travellers and pilgrims to Gare de la Louvre

Aboard the bright train; each clutching a docket
Crowded isolation; beware the pick pocket
Swoops from the blackness, then groans to a halt
Staccato sharp echoes; swift heels flee the vault

As midnight is sounded; chilled silence descends
Alone on the platform a bundle unbends
A stiff ragged mummy in two overcoat skins
The bagman is moving; his night's vigil begins

R H Cowley

SAD SALFORD LAD

Take a lump of rough tough stuff
Squeeze between your fingers
Do so till it cries - enough
Killing any hope that lingers

Stuff it in a sky-high flat
Above the city sights so mad
And when you've finished doing that
You've made a young sad Salford lad

T Levy

9

AUTUMN/WINTER

Purple and red,
The poor dead heads
Of bright fuschia
Drip onto the cold
Grey road below

And the sun's rays
Weakening,
Waver uncertain
Through autumn mists.
Summer must go.

And gusty winds
Gaining strength
Drag leaves unwillingly
From branches.
Chilling bone.

And soon winter
Will descend,
Cold and bleak.
Freezing bare earth
Like stone.

Chérianne Wren

MUSIC

Music gently flows along
Each note travels with pride and song
Knows no boundaries young or old
Creating pictures to unfold

Music from cultures near and far
A language all may understand
Granting wishes of love and beauty
Never ceasing to do its duty

Listen with beauty
And stillness and hush
As the notes come gently flowing
Amidst a hectic world of rush

Melissa Victoria Sarah Warrilow (15)

HARVEST TIME

Misty mornings rich with dew
Golden days with skies of blue
Twilight brings an evening cool
   Harvest time is here.

Crops are lifted from the ground
Straw stacks rising big and round
Grain in sacks to warehouse bound
   Harvest time is here.

Berries glisten round and black
Jam to make and jars to stack
Freeze the peas and beans in packs
   Harvest time is here.

Squirrels gather in their hoard
Logs are cut and stacked and stored
Wine in casks and bottles poured
   Harvest time is here.

Bonfire smoke drifts in the air
Field mice scurry here and there
And reaping's done with time to spare
   Harvest time is here.

From the church bells do ring
All the choirs on earth do sing
Gifts to God the people bring
   Harvest time is here.

Hazel Crellin

LOVE LINES

Hold me again
If there is time
Enough before you
Sleep or leave or die;
Hold me like a stone
Carved as one form,
Made to outlast
The vagaries of mood
And age and change.
Clamp me to you
In this one moment
We are both alive together.

Later, when I look back,
The shadow that spoiled
Your face, slanting
Like a web of glass,
So fine as to seem
A trick of the light,
May never have been
In just that place,
But cast elsewhere
By clouds across
An undressed moon.

Hold me again
Before I hurt you
With my nature
Or you grow silent
In a separate chair;
Turn your face
To the light for me,
Smile with your eyes
If you are able.

Hold me again
While there is still time
Before you sleep
Or leave or die -
In this one moment,
Cold by the opening door,
In this one moment
We are both alive together.

Deborah Casson

UNTITLED

Oh it's hard to be a poet in a week
When your mental outlook's overcast
And general forecast's bleak
But here I go I'll draw the curtains of my mind
In seven days I'll re-incarnate
And emerge poet sublime

Hang on -

There's been no recent bereavement or nought to take away my breath
And indeed the very thought of it just frightens me to death
I can picture distant pastures petals twirling in the breeze
Enough to bring a full grown man a crashing to his knees
Or lovers young entwined amidst some wild exotic caper
But what I'd really like to do is put it down on paper

Though wait - I feel it coming to the surface of my mind
Oh damn it's gone away again - perhaps another time

Alas this poet business is a wee bit overrated
Instead of rapturous prose aflow I only get frustrated

When you're just a meagre typist and you've no artistic streak
And your note left for the milkman was the novel of the week
It's time to look inside your brain and utilise what's in it
Then it emerges so profound - I'll stick to typing minutes!

Anon

THE SOUND OF THE SOUND

A fisherman told me, when he was a boy,
He walked thro' Cregneish seaward bound,
And high on the cliffs looking out to the Calf,
He heard the sound of the Sound, he said,
He heard the sound of the Sound,
And the voices clear on a summer's day,
That tried to steal the child away.

The sirens sang in the turbulent sea,
And the rocks made their voices resound,
The boy was bewitched by the music he heard,
Oh! The plaintive sound of the Sound, he said,
The plaintive sound of the Sound,
And the voices clear on a summer's day,
That tried to steal the child away.

'Twas then that the gulls in a mocking rebuke,
Joined in as they circled around,
And spoiled the song he was desperate to hear,
The mystical sound of the Sound, he said,
The mystical sound of the Sound,
And the voices clear on a summer's day,
That almost stole the child away.

Thro' many long years, he returns to that spot,
And sits on the cool, green Manx ground,
For one day, he tells me, he'll hear them again,
And answer the call of the Sound, he says,
The magical sound of the Sound,
And the voices clear on a summer's day,
Will steal a tired old man away.

Paula Scatchard

1945

I can still feel the closeness of her
The feel of her heart beating steady
I can still smell the freshness of her
strawberry blonde hair, the loveliness
of my Mother
The knock on the door, jumping out of the
bed, peeping through the curtain looking
down on a soldier's head, the smile as he
lifted his face towards mine.
The khaki overcoat the haversack that hung
on his shoulder, was this strange man the father
I never knew? Up in the air he swung me so high
When he held the strawberry blonde so tight I wanted
to cry. Would he stay long I wanted to know? Yes I
was told forever. So no more would I feel snug and
warm in bed with my darling mother and smell the
freshness of her strawberry blonde hair

Patricia Prior

FRIEND
(Dedicated to Steven Helwich)

Will you look down upon me and keep me far from harm,
If at times I stray from protection then pick me up and take me in your arms,
Guide me and teach me in any way you know,
Direct me to true friends and avoid all foe,
Help me find hope in my darkest moments of despair,
Shine faith's light and let me know you're there,
Above us, beyond us, out of sight and touch,
But cherished memories of you are held tight in my soul's clutch.
Understanding a friend has gone forever is the hardest thing to do,
Especially one that was as close and admired as you,
So take care of me please until my last day draws to its end,
So I'll be allowed in where you are and we'll be together again, friend.

K Reilly

15

SWALLOWS

The swallow skims over the river
The swallow flies over the grass,
The wind sets the grass all a quiver
The water is shattered like glass.

The swallow looks into the window
The swallow's reflection looks out,
She hesitates only a moment
And instantly turns all about.

The swallow flies into the stables
The nests from last year are still there,
High in the roof under the gables
Just waiting for her to appear.

The garden is full of small swallows
All happily learning to fly,
One moment she leads and then follows,
Swooping low and then soaring on high.

There is a slight change in the weather
Summer's nearly over I fear.
The swallows have gone, not forever
Because they'll be back here next year.

Heather Currey

LIFE TRAIN

Out in the cold away from it all
Ponder on the thoughts of yesteryear
Until reality's knife cuts deeper
Slicing the dreams you try to cling to
The memories now on celluloid.
Cutter pastes the good times over bad
And gloss to make the past seem better
Than the reality of this harsh hour.

16

Watch as it fades to reality
A train that pulls silently away
And leaves you on a distant station
Far from the destination of your youth
And waiting for the next to take you
Yet further from the mainline lifeline
Out on a branch out on a limb.

Clickety clack train on the track
The runaway train of your childhood
No looking back and no turning back
Estranged from the citizens of home
That only knew you before you left
To start a new life out in the cold.

J H Ayres

FULL MOON

I raised the moon to my lips
as it lay on its table of sky,
then licked it white of my wishes
until it caught the lost light from your eye.

Each night I watched it grow smaller
against the gloom above, passively blind.
A plate that halved and divided,
then left me, like love had, behind.

Better perhaps, if though separate,
tiny and flung far afield,
to have bet on the thousands of stars, constant
as kisses, that yet light the love they once sealed.

Norma Winearls

THE WATER FLOWS ON

He stands and gazes down below
and watches the water go to and fro,
alone at night on bridge he stands
holding on with feeble hands.
His heart is torn his mind adrift, his life
has ceased no more to give.

What could be torturing his aching brain
to make him think that this is sane,
what could have caused this hour of grief
to bring this feeling of such disbelief.
No one can tell only he for it's his private misery.

He turns his head for one last look
the city sleeps with stars above,
no one in sight, no one to know,
no one to plead for him not to go.
He scoops the tears from round his eyes and
erects his head to the sky,
'Oh God, oh God, that I should die,'
his words echo on. But now the bridge is empty
as the water flows on.

T R Slaney

THE END OF TIME

An island at the end of Time - deserted now but once replete
with family, and homestead built of stone; a place of warmth, complete
with sheep and goats that on this isle spent their peaceful days,
away from mainland cares, their own lives the silent world belays.

But now, inhabited by seabirds, seals and native four-horned sheep,
this land seems in its solitude to be asleep.
Yet pounded by the waves it remains supreme
a clefted shoreline protects its sward of green.

18

It seems but just a step across the Sound
of waters blue, yet with a roaring round
the islet Kitterland, its lighthouse lone and still.
Nothing stirs the peace but cry of seabirds raucous, shrill.

Occasionally, a foreign foot will tread its paths to find
a home of gulls, though mainly it is seen by human-kind
in passing boats who ride the waves around its rocky shore,
a place of calm and isolate; an idyll rarely seen before.

Where is this land, afar, in some stranger clime,
across the ocean wide, where one must fly in altered time?
No! This the end of earth in God's creative Plan,
The Calf, the island at the foot of Mann.

Ray Oldham

NATURE'S SENTRY

The owl sits in a gap in the wall
Watching over his domain to call.
Too wit awoo, too wit awoo.
He looks like the keeper who misses naught
His actions are instinct never taught.
He resides in a ruin or hole in a tree
He's one of Nature's Sentry's.
As darkness falls the hoot owl calls
Too wit a woo. Too wit awoo.
The mouse feigns death as he falls
He is majestic like a king.
His music in the forest sings
He is the keeper of the night.
His large eyes shine like a beam so bright
So when dusk falls and night-time comes around
Stop and listen for the hoot owls sound
As he swoops to catch his prey off the ground.

J Oung

19

TYNWALD DAY

Every year, in early July,
on the Isle of Man the flags all fly;
A public holiday is proclaimed
for *Tynwald Day* as it is named.
Lengthy plans are put in hand
for celebrations throughout the land.
At St John's - where the ceremony takes place -
A canopy, tiered seats, and bunting fill the space
where, when the proceedings do begin,
all the island dignitaries will process in,
to take their seats on the staggered mound,
the centrepiece of this revered ground.
Officers, Ministers, Clergy and Deemsters
in traditional dress - some with gaiters -
leave fleets of cars to enter God's House
where serenity reigns, all as quiet as a mouse.
Outside the bands are playing as the Governor arrives
with the Lord of Man's representative by his side.
After a short service which is relayed to the masses
they all make their way over the strewn rushes
to sit and hear the years laws promulgated
and see petitioners hand grievances which have waited
for this day when they can be handed in
to be considered and judged, hopefully to win.
When the official photographer has recorded the day
to Government House the crowds make their way.
It's summertime and the grounds look aglow
the lawns, flowers and ladies fashions, all on show.
The Isle of Man has notched up another year
of the self governing freedom its citizens hold so dear.

Barbara Vian

'TWAS JUST A DREAM

'Twas just a dream
Of fantasy
That never would come true.

To meet the best
And stand the test
In combat with the few.

And yet the will
Of men of steel
Would surely come to pass.

When through the gates
Of Lords they'd walk
Onto the hallowed grass.

The road was long
The battle hard
For victory to earn.

But as the nineties
Beckoned
The tide began to turn.

And now the dream's
Reality
For all the world to see.

No longer
Outside looking in
But true equality.

Consolidation
Will be done
A learning process plan.

A future bright
Is waiting
For every Durham man.

Tony Sheldon

SWEET HEARTBREAK

Sweet heartbreak, leave me now
Your timing is false
I am not ready for you.

My chest is on fire, flames
Not cleansing, but consuming
Torturing me with me memories,

Old thoughts seeping, slowly dripping
Pooling then vanishing
Through the blackened husk of my heart.

The fire spreads, taking over,
Rational thoughts forgotten
Ashes only left to remind.

This pain is not caused by one, but two,
Righteous self-pity
Does not help to douse the flames.

But I cannot let this happen
Watch everything crumble
Turn into dust.

Sweet heartbreak, leave me now
Your timing is false
I will not accept you.

Lee James Quaggin

UNTITLED

It shrouds us with its offerings
Challenges our lives, disrupts our routines
And shadows our days!
Sometimes mild, often fierce
But always present.

We can become trapped -
As water is inside a tap.
We can hide in our living shells
And wait for its anger to calm
So we do not come to any harm.

The weather!
What is this extreme factor
Extreme being . . . extreme existence?
            The weather!

Jayne Marie Mottram

THE WALL OF DEPRESSION, THEN FREEDOM

We all make mistakes yes, we all have a wall.
The wall is made up of bricks.
At times without realising we are trapped inside
The surroundings of the wall.
OK, we are given a cement mixer, a shovel and a tap,
Also sand and cement mix.
Right when things are not going so good the wall starts falling down,
We then with a lot of effort, cement back the bricks which have fallen,
But the harder we try the bricks begin to decay.

Do you really need this wall break through the old bricks,
The decayed and crumbled ones,
Push through and a light is in front of you.
You made it, leave the wall behind, it's hard agreed!

You were once behind that wall, now you are free
The green fresh field in front of you.
Keep running until in the distance the wall disappears.
You're not alone because we all have a wall,
When the wall starts to come back you crumble
With it but tell yourself and remember break free!
Yes you can, and it has been done.

Joanne Faragher

MANCHESTER'S TRAM

Petrol fumes they pen and ink
This has made me start to think
Manchester's trams will be a God send
If they start a popular trend
Lower pollution in the British Isles
Will encourage grandchildrens' smiles
And should the trams ever break down
There's another solution can be found
Horse-drawn trams could become the rage
Bringing back a bygone age
The horses would be a novelty you know
And what they leave behind would make the roses grow.

K Slingo

MIDDLETON NOSTALGIA

Today I look at Middleton and see another town,
A place where, if you lived outside, you had to travel down.
Each hill led out to foreign towns like Oldham, Rochdale, Bury.
To get across the river Irk do I recall a ferry?
The bluebells colouring Alki Woods, the brass band in the park,
I get into nostalgic moods when dozing in the dark.
Fishing in Rhodes lodges where grey tiddlers were caught,
Pages' corner shop where tuppenny ice-lollies were bought,
Wakes week holiday when you couldn't buy your shopping
'Cause all the shops were shut, their owners off to Blackpool popping.
Walking Day, girls dressed in white, banners flying high,
Onlookers on Wood Street cheering as the band went by.
The fountain in the gardens amid the beds of flowers
Where local folk could meet and chat and pass away the hours.
Forget the white fluff on dark coats, the chimneys belching smoke
The fumes from mills, the foggy days that almost made you choke.
The Middleton I think about is friendly and sincere,
That cannot change like buildings have, with every passing year.

J Davis

ALEXANDRA PARK LAKE

Only black stone
Statues capturing only the blackness
Of the soul,
Watch her.
Her sandalled brown feet
Break the glass threads of frozen grass
And scratch blue blood
From her weak skin.

Voices . . . Voices . . .
Voices of the night.
Suspended
In mid sentence;
Waiting for the thaw.
Like her fingers,
The membranes of her cheeks,
Knotted by seams of blue frost;
She nears the ink-still waters.

She thinks the glitter of ice,
Is her cracked destinies
Hiding the colours of
Their nakedness.
Her head raises to challenge the starless sky
And she waits for a sign.

There is no sign.
The colours of her destinies cut the depth
As they cut through her tired flesh.
The morning found the ruin of her lips and eyes
Hidden in the stillness that was her death.

The voices of the night are filled
With the silence of her sleep.

Farah Shaheen

MANCHESTER CITY MIRAGE

The sunlight dances on the water,
The ducks glide across the lake,
The swan swims straight and tall.
(And humans build a world of hate.)

Flat capped, silvered hair, men amble,
Lovers smile, and walk hand in hand,
Children hide and seek in trees.
(And slowly we devastate the land.)

In this Manchester City mirage,
Civilised Cornucopia,
I feel an uneasy peace.
(And so many are ruled by fear.)

How can I be at peace
When God's world is warring?
How can I be at peace
When God's world is dying?
How can I be at peace
When God's out there crying?

Those tears fall unnoticed by all,
As they enjoy the first warm spell,
Playing, walking, loving park.
(And the earth is turned into hell).

David Hardman

CHESHIRE LIFE

Cheshire is a wonderful little pearl in England
Stately wood, plains, hills, rivers, salt and sand.
Friendly villages are found down winding lanes
Many homes still are seen with roofs of thatch,
Fields throughout the summer yield up their grains
Quaint old fashioned market towns have no match.

A cathedral, castles with moats, a burial ground
Black and white houses, open air markets all to be found.
The grin of the Cheshire Cat is so well known
Famous too is of course that delicious Cheshire cheese
Morris and maypole dancing are not alone
Country dancing is also done with ease.

P M H Wood

OLDHAM

Driving up from Manchester,
Or down from Saddleworth Moor,
Either way, you just can't help
Knocking on *Oldham's* door,
The tough old days of cobbled streets
And smoky factory walls,
Are in the past, those days are gone,
And wearing clogs and shawls,
It's had a lot of face-lifts
This small industrial town,
So if you've time, bide awhile,
And have a look around,
We've buildings to be proud of
Some old and some quite new,
And our famous outside market,
Takes some beating too,
You'll find the natives friendly,
And I'm sure you'll call again,
In spite of what they say down south,
It doesn't always *rain* . . .

Annie Campbell

OLDHAM RUNS ALL DAY

This crowded town of Oldham runs all day,
Its population thrives on work and play;
Who cares if slave-earned cash is thrown away,
In this gay town of Oldham?

The place is swarmed with walking doll coquettes,
And long haired youths with patterned epaulettes;
The over sixty flirts have no regrets
In this fleet town of Oldham.

Our fashionable matrons like to share
The modern trend, they choose their outdoor wear
To tally with the colour of their hair,
In this proud town of Oldham.

All types of cars are seen on every hand,
Some carry guests, some carry contraband;
Drug addicts trade here too, I understand,
In this rash town of Oldham.

We find employment for the healthy man,
And for afflicted people, when we can,
In truth, we boast a general working plan
In this deft town of Oldham.

Sarah A Hunter

MANCHURIAN PRIDE

Manchester a site picked by Romans to put up their
tents, a place that was known of wherever they
went. A place that was chosen for its rivers for
trade and so it expanded, a city was made. Cotton
was mostly its means to survive and so many grew
rich, but the poor often died. For health was quite
damaged by long hours and smogs, has the cobbled
streets rang to those worker's clogs.

These days for it's football and rain it is known far
and wide, industrial boom it has took in its stride.
Famous its sons for inventions and art, even one of
them gave the atom a start. Twentieth century
brings even more praise, for now comes the
Complex, Europe's biggest place, to bring here
together from near and far the athletes, the sportsmen
all ready to spar.

No more coughing and sputtering for the youth of
these streets, just a panting and sweating with the
chance to compete in the sports of their choice, in
the place where they live and so a great thank you
we all then should give to the ones who made
Manchester grow from the grime, to a now famous
city, our Manchurian's pride.

B A Clayton

WHIT WALK IN GREENFIELD

'Left, right, left . . .
Here, hang on a minute, which is my left?'
A crafty glance to the right:
'Oh, I see, that foot.
No, that's still not right.
A quick skip then, that should do it.
No, still wrong.
Perhaps I put my shoes on the wrong feet this morning,
That might be why they're going wrong.
'Hi ya!'
Oops, not supposed to wave,
I forgot.
Ow! It's not my fault I walked up your legs,
You should have said you'd stopped.
Well, I didn't want to come anyway,
But mum made me!'

Maggie Rich

29

NEWTON HEATH REMEMBERED

I remember the old days before slum-clearance
we had landmarks
like our own town hall with its clock tower,
pubs on corners, up the road as far as Church Street.
and we had shops.
and Jones's pawn-shop, and the Co-op, and chip shops (English),
there were corner shops where we bought on tick
and we had cinemas (three).
and wireless, and library books, and public wash-baths,
and the wash-house where we took our washing,
unless you did your own with a tub,
and a mangle with big wooden rollers.
some houses still had gas lights with mantels;
doorsteps were still donkey-stoned, and rag-and-bone men called,
and we had neighbours.
there were cobbles and tram-lines and horse muck on the road,
and buildings were soot-blackened,
and we had fog.
there were factories where people worked,
and mills full of chattering girls,
and we had jobs.
we had Whitsuntide processions and we cheered the bands,
especially the Top Hat Band,
and everyone wore their new clothes,
and we had Sunday Schools.
and Manchester holidays, end of July, to Blackpool,
and Wilson's and Dean's charas did day-trips to Morecambe or Rhyl.
we ate potato pie, steak and cow-heel, and tripe,
and we were in Lancashire, not Greater Manchester,
and we had pride.

Alan Smith

SATURDAY NIGHT, SUNDAY MORNING

Lovers
steal their private moment near pub brawl
Rivers
zig-zag down as urine from club walls
Chortles
one fat landlord at his balance sheet
Bottles
smashed in rage (bravado) in the street
Sick cracks
echoing down Yorkshire Street in rhyme
Six-packs
emptied by a party after time
Fissures
sported by young lads with stitches neat
Tissues
soggy, bloodied, lying on cab seats
Glass
everywhere, and grounded down like sugar
Sparse
are taxis to escape the side-street mugger
Swishy lads
blunder from shop doorways, pants all stained
Shish kebabs
regurgitant on pavements in the rain
Burger
sits congealing on the pub's worn sill
Lager
stands nearby, dilute, forgotten, still
Oldham
fades in pale, like sick-faced drunks from sleep
Hoodlum
left this mess for someone else to sweep.

Scott Richardson

CLOGS AND CANALS

Clogs and canals and sky-scraper flats,
Football and rugby and flat nebber caps,
The Beatles, McCartney, Lennon and George,
Ringo, the Mersey, the old river barge,
The Liver bird, Blackpool, the Tower and lights,
Winter hill, Holcombe, magnificent sights,
Granada, and chip shops, and hot mushy peas,
Trotters, black puddings, and Lancashire cheese,
Wigan, the pier, the absence of mines,
Headgears, and chimneys, and coal wagon lines,
Memories of cobbles, and coal dust, and pies,
Kayli and licorice, and stars in my eyes,
Now I am older, wind's blown away youth,
But my compass still points to the home of truth,
For my mind holds a magnet, it's been there from the start,
And it's pulling me home to the truth in my heart.

Sally James

THE FOX

Pressed against the bushes.
He creeps silently past.
Suddenly he stops, and listens
His ears pricked and head high,
His reddish coat and long bushy tail,
Are caught in the moonlight.
He stands, his glossy black eyes glistening,
He barks and in the distant woods,
A reply!
Then he dashes off, a reddish rusty streak,
Into the woodland and away,
Until the darkness swallowed him up.
And all is quiet.

Julia Yates

FALCON COTTAGE

Falcon Cottage has swellings in its side
From the slow weight of planets,
The long, allowed embrace,
That costs rubble in the close.
It has eyelid, lapping thatch,
And its fringe is a lacing to the skies.
Beyond, the sandstone ridge is robbed of age,
It pours the gantry gorse,
Going into yellow,
Lauding sun,
While the same beams buckle.
In the drift, we should snag a knot in
Its noble inspiration,
Lest the sand lands say.

The magpie buildings
That strut the Cheshire soil,
Seem brief to be,
Capable of a ship's sinking,
In what holds as haste.
They are blunt mirrors
Before our frame filled eyes.

Peter Beswick

THE WHITE LADY

Full moon midnight Marbury motorbike home.
No street lights light my way.
Headlight fades when speed drops.

Marbury Park's reputedly haunted and the
darkness ignites my imagination. I scare
myself to death as a mirrored moon reveals
her face behind me!

Philip Johnson

WITCHES

Mid to South
        you can almost smell the brine.

Winnington factories jagged and visible
against the skyline,
I'm stood near the boatlift, looking down.
Smoke billowing, joining hands with the clouds.

North, Middle and Nant;
the Witches are everywhere, casting spells,
luring the unsuspecting in.
They are white, not black.

By the River Weaver some houses
perch on a bay of brine,
be careful yours is not spirited away
by those quiet witches.

They make no sound,
the towns gently sink unawares
and everyone does their shopping,
drinks in pubs, go to churches.

Mid to South,
        you can almost smell the brine.
Leaves a salty taste in your mouth.

Nikky Martin

THE ANDERTON LIFT

How sad, how sad, the sombre lift now idly stands
Looking dejected, expressionless, without a face
Created by man's own ingenious hands
Yet left to rot upon its skeletal base.

This towering monument, an integral part of local history
Neglected for so long as dwindling profits raced
But not erased from the canal users' memory
With the fight for restoration committed and embraced

So the lift now waits with future hope once more
To see those laden caissons proudly rise and fall
We have to find the money and totally restore
This piece of Cheshire heritage, preserved for one and all.

Andrew Treble

THE STREETS OF CHESTER

Busy streets
Winter fleets
Feet patter up and down
Cobbles

Sandstone walls
Marble halls
The curfew bell chimes
On the 9th hour

People coming
People going
All the time
Toing and froing

I wonder what they have
On their minds
Perhaps one day
Peace and happiness
They'll find.

Beverley A Powell

A LITTLE POEM OF A CHESHIRE COUNTRY COTTAGE

It's a lovely old cottage in a quiet country lane
Not mentioned in history of thought of in fame
But a relic so true of our dear countryside
It's near to a woodland of bracken and trees
Makes the loveliest landscape you ever have seen
And when it is night and the bird songs are done
The rabbits come out and don't they have fun
But the next thing you hear, is a scuffle and rush
Mr Reynard's popped out from round a big bush
And when in the summer, the sun being so hot
You just loll in the shade, and don't care a jot
So beware all ye townspeople, that pass by this day
Take the frown from your face, and smile all the way
It's just a piece of old England, not far from a town
And they wouldn't change places with you for a crown
A little church you will find, not too far away
Where the people they go, to kneel, and to pray
So farewell dear old cottage, we must wend on our way
Leaving a relic of old England, in glory to stay.

John Newton

REMEMBRANCE

The time has come to bow our heads,
To remember all the nation's dead,
The game was war, the price was paid,
By people loyal to the grave
Their deeds are past, their time has gone
Only their memory lingers on
The years may come, the years may go.
Today we mourn, those loved ones so.

Marion H Liddle

CHESHIRE PLAIN

Flat fields, tessellated, chequerboard, a patchwork quilt,
Ribbon strands of green and grey and indigo retreating into the haze.
Mirror flashes of pond and marsh,
Criss-crossing waterways and ditches,
Pied mosaics of Friesian herds imperceptibly changing formation hour
by hour.

Small sturdy oaks scattered along the fretwork hedgerows,
Florets of bunchy dark foliage lining the pale green squares,
All upward growth dwarfed by the vast arable flatness.
Towering metal pylons, cables of unimaginable weight
Bewitched to gossamer threads of lace mincing across grass and furrow,
Mighty concrete chimneys belching steam fade to thumbprint smudges
set in rows.

Contorted undulating pipes of steel intestine reduced to silver filigree
Winking and blinking in the watery sunshine.

Turn and let your gaze sweep all around.
Find focus and relief in stark Helsby Hill, charcoal silhouette against a
white paper sky.

In the ancient outcrops and cresting sandstone ridge.
Beeston, Peckforton, Bickerton, Burwardsley.
The foaming woods of high summer,
Oak and chestnut creaming down the gentle slopes,
Scots pines standing dark sentinel above farms and winding lanes.
Rocky crags of burnt scar black and gritty red
Still sheer above a dim memory of prehistoric seas
Which seeped against the livid undercliff,
An ocean floor, mother to this stretching verdant plain.

And to the West, beyond the placid, shining Dee
The blue Welsh hills beckon with the promise of a wilder, hidden land.

Jenny Brockley

AMIDST THE RUINS

Whenever I feel like getting away,
Away from life's daily hassle.
I jump in the car and spend the day,
Amidst the ruins of Beeston Castle.
I walk around for hours
Admiring this ancient site.
I marvel at its towers,
Its stone turrets, portcullis and height.

As I walk along the *Hollow Way*
A feeling of peace comes over me.
My worries in life are kept at bay,
In this place of tranquillity.
The outer gatehouse I walk under,
On my way up to the keep.
I look around in awesome wonder
At this fortress with its history so deep.

I carry on up the hill,
Towards the castle itself.
I must admit it is a thrill,
Now I've seen it for myself.
This monument so worn with age,
Is our legacy forever.
It has witnessed the results of violent rage,
Of man's every evil endeavour.

Now it stands so silent,
perched upon a giant rock.
Standing so defiant,
Against history's cruel clock.
For this heirloom of our county
Handed down over centuries gone by,
Is our reward; our bounty
And will never ever die.

Charles Doherty

PAST RETURNS

I close my eyes and drift to times
Of Cheshire as a child.
As clear as Summer morn, names return
To form places; places to form names.
Woodbine Cottage,. Dingley Dell, Bluebell Wood
Places still remain, names change.
Hares in bogs white tipped copper brush.
Water cress cut from crystal streams.
Brocks Hollow, sets of years before
Skylarks trill, bees hum, the unmistakable
Smell of the Weaver; infrequent mechanical sound,
Places still remain, names change.
Acton Lodge, place of my birth
Safe solid red brick, always to be home
Still standing, not changed.
Places change, names return.

James S Clarke

MERSEY VIEW REVISITED

Sunday school trips in the fifties
Swing-boats, ice-cream, lemonade,
Slot-machines and helter-skelter,
Picnic in a heathery glade.

Return nostalgic in the nineties,
Modern brick monstrosity.
Cinder car-park, where's the grass gone?
So called progress? Tragedy.

Jenni J Moores

NATURE TRAIL

Mist shrouded night on miles of green meadow
Gives way very slowly to dawn's golden glow,

Blossoms of hawthorn some pink and some white
Paint pastel shades on morning's bright light,

Songs from dawn's chorus drift tree to tree
Such is the beauty all around to see,

Willows weep to the clear water's edge
Oft' rippled by swans with gift of royal pledge,

Sandy hills clothed with flowers wild and blue
Cascading brooks dance with silver-white hue,

Quiet then the forest with many a wide glade
Leads to lush meadow nature's wealth to amaze.

John A Harris

AROUND COLSHAW

Yonder the horizon changes fast
                the bypass looms - it's power is cast -
Bygone RAF camps - skeleton no more - all gone!
Empty schools we remember -
                buildings we could see -
The wand has been waved -
                car parks arise -
There's shops - a store - and a
                Wilmslow that flies -
Where it was green - now it is white -
It'll never need watering - to get thro" the night -
The traffic is heavy - it roars with distress -
Where it all comes from - is anyone's guess -
At least we know now -
                it'll soon be going!

Norbert Atherton

LANDMARKS

Cheshire, undisclosed, serene,
Like a dreaming ancient queen,
Seeing what will and has been.

Once beneath sea-level
Beeston crag dropped by the Devil,
Dirge and revel,

Salt mines of the Roman,
Full of evil omen,
To the Yeoman.

Wirral wild and weird,
Where Gawain feared,
And cheered,

Peckforton
Answering Beeson,
Thurstaton.

Bunbury still the same as ever
How ever
Could one sever

Wilde from wit
Or never sit
Beside the pit

In Christleton where swans glide,
On the water made a slide,
In winter or decide,

In Parkgate on which ice-cream flavour
To sit and savour
Where Emma Hamilton lived until a braver

Man she met,
Gaze across the broad Dee estuary and forget
To fret.

Anne Beatty

41

BREATHING IN CHESHIRE

'Aye by gum', said John Bry's Mum
'Doesn't it look glum?'
'Why no' said John Bry
'It's glorious July'
And the breeze in the trees
Swirled around their knees
Said John Bry 'It's so much fresher
Here in lovely Cheshire'.
Mum gave a sigh and almost asked why
Her youngest son, John Bry
For a country born farmer,
Oh such a charmer!
No matter what inside
He never could hide
That Cheshire Cat grin
Which beamed from within!

Lisa Jones

A SEEING FRIEND

Four o'clock, it's time to go
Through the town I've come to know.
Because my master's blind you see,
So I know he relies on me,
To take him through the Chester streets
To the bus stop where he meets -
People waiting for their bus
They move back make way for us.
Here's the bus, I know the smell,
I'll guide him on, he copes so well.
Soon we're home, it's time for tea,
I'm glad I help my friend to see.

Pamela Pickford

CHESHIRE'S TRIPLE CROWN

Wallasey and Winsford, Nantwich and Crewe,
Waiting for a train - maybe for two,
In Cheshire's vale royal, greener grass does not grow,
Nor not lose its sheaves, nor its own show.

Northwich, New Brighton - Alderley its edge
'Ere up north, there's nought but good 'edge'
And good fields too and cattle besides,
For Cheshire's greenest vale is twixt the Dee's side.

Bulkeley and Burwardsley, Dunham on the hill,
What fine Cheshire names, it's the earth that they till.

Yet Cheshire's main city was once a port,
A carrier of cargo save except this of nought,
Straddling the kingdom, as Ms Gaskell once wrote,
Good Charles lost the north but should rightly gloat.
Lions make leopards tame, yet not lose their spots!
For Cheshire itself loves its raindrops,.
As here, in the main, farming's the king,
From Wallasey to Winsford, as in Nantwich as in Crewe.

Sebastian Beatty

THIS NON TAKEN HEART

Oh, I am the heart not taken
The one thought not worth breaking.
I am the late blooming rose
With only my strongest dreams to hold
On this less travelled road.
Who really knows . . .
Maybe the hearts not taken
Are truly made of gold.

Neil Joseph Massey

DO IT! (AFTER A VISIT TO A CHESHIRE DAIRY FARM)

Friesian cows
Black and white
And dirty.
They're not particular, cows.
they don't mind where or when they
do it!
They just lift up their tails and
do it!
Whether eating,
Whether milking,
Whether standing,
Whatever, however, they just
do it!
Like stone thrown into a pond
Plop, plop, plop!
Anywhere, anytime they just
do it!

Phil Adlington

GROSVENOR PARK

I often walk your trammelled ways,
        when days are heavy and my heart is cold;
for in your colour and your gaiety
        I find my substitute and my sanctuary.

On your paths, on your stones
        I find peace, I find joy;
for all my roads converge on woe
        while yours divert and laughter meet.

Come spring, come summer
        I bring winter snow,
and within the span of an hour,
        it melts, and restores a glow.

And people come, and people see,
        this church built on the Dee;
from all the shadows in the land,
        displaced beneath this tulip by God's own hand.

So dance with the poplars, and sing with the lark;
        of all the holy places, in this holy ark,
I give you my one, my one guarantee of heart,
        this murmuring, tranquil park.

Simon Francis

TRIBUTE TO TRISTAN JONES

A full storm ahead wet the new babes head off the island that bore his name
The life that he led was the book that I read which put my life to shame.

The first breath he drew was of the ocean that blew through the porthole
        in the steamer.
The stories he told as he grew old were food for this poor dreamer.

He grew brave and strong as the years came along and sailed with the
        Navy before;
buying a boat he ventured afloat with a one eyed, three legged Labrador.

He sailed all the seas and sailed up the Andes and his Incredible
        Voyage became:
the source of a book which an Editor took and it brough him
        world-wide fame.

So I wrote this poem, although I didn't know him because the books that
        he wrote that I read.
They brought adventures to me, as I sat on the settee.
Now I'm ever so sorry cos he's dead.

Jennifer Marshall

THROUGH A CHESHIRE SCENE

Through pretty villages, shady lanes,
  On a fine day let us wander awhile,
Always looking at the lovely view,
  Then sitting leg-swinging on a stile.

We can say: 'What is more delightful?'
  Meandering through a Cheshire scene,
Where gentle cattle and fine sheep graze,
  In pastures tranquil and verdant green.

Happy to be healthily free,
  Horses - flying manes - frisking playfully,
Loving their young riders without stint,
  Who ride them expertly, skilfully.

Gazing, one can see in the distance
  Down in the valley there stands a mill.
It is a museum nowadays:
  The machinery has long been still.

Cheshire has a long, proud history,
  For all its quiet and gentle calm.
Cheshire bowmen were highly renowned:
  They saw that great kings came to no harm.

Bloody battles were fought on stained earth;
  Great castles, a-top hills, were held to siege.
Roundheads made their last stand and then won:
  Cavaliers - who tried to save their liege.

Listen! the old church clock is striking:
  We know it is a quarter to three.
Soon, my friend, we'll do no more walking.
  Anticipation! It'll be time for tea.

J Millington

OWLEY WOOD'S MAGIC

The water trickling through the stream,
And the sun beating down, makes me feel in a dream.
The sounds of the cuckoo, high up in the tree,
Squirrels and woodpeckers are my company.
The scent of bluebells is in the air,
As butterflies go by, without a care.
I stroll along, through clumps of celandine,
As I seem to lose all sense of time.
And when summer fades and autumn calls,
Chestnuts start falling in their prickly balls.
I wander through the leafy mounds,
A dog rushes by in leaps and bounds.
It's time to go home, as dusk starts to fall,
I finally hear an odd owl's call.
Oh! what a joy to walk through Owley Wood,
I'd come every day - if only I could!

Diane Kryger-Collins

CHESHIRE

Rolling, endless countryside with many shades of green
Leafy lanes and bridle paths to interweave the scene
Canals which meander through golden fields of wheat
The lock gates make the traveller a very welcome seat
Whilst watching swifts and martins circling lazily overhead
Or the heron standing motionless, then with one flick of his head
His lunch is caught and swallowed up and all is peace again
Cheshire seen through my eyes is a green and pleasant lane

Iola D Norbury

CHESTER CATHEDRAL

See Hugh's design nine hundred years ago,
His title held by Charles today.
Two hundred years before there were interred
The bones of Werburgh, nun now sanctified,
Ousting St Peter to the Cross.
Slowly the Abbey rose,
The tower completed with a steeple planned.
At the fourth century came Dean John:
The West front rose, the Choir Aisle splayed out.
Then were thrown out the Abbot and his monks
To fund the whim of a connubial King.
Yet consolation chanced - a school
Named for the King, which housed eight choristers.
The later Cromwell sent no trooper out
For havoc, as on other godly stones.
Year after year was spent by Thomas Brook,
The Dean, in earnest labour for repair.
The building now rose great but gaunt,
A fortress symbolising God's defence.
What shall we say of Gilbert Scott?
Those tiny turrets torturing the sky,
In tune with his time but no more with ours,
Which Addleshaw now represents,
The Dean who built a tower for bells
Too weighty for the central loft;
Yes, new in shape, but harmonising well
With all the labour of nine hundred years.
If contemplation of a steeple stays
Pray God that it be grand and tall,
Pointing a sure way up.

W Scott

THE AMPHITHEATRE

I cast back my immortal eye
        two thousand years ago,
and this quiet half circle - passed by buses now
        was then a circle of blood.

Upon the wall, that now divides the ring,
        once a caesar stood,
with feasting eyes and howling cries,
        amongst the gore he stood.

The 'palling scene which now plays host,
        to tourists and ice cream,
caesar showed his imperial thrall -
        his purple thumb did fall -

There the crowd did roar -
        - and women shouted more
to see the sticky swords
        pull living cord from cord.

Wouldn't it be sublime - and yes, a sin I know
        to cast this ridiculous lot,
with Nippon cameras and falling gut -
        back to the crowd, the crimson ruck?

Hear the bear and hear the lion, following dog and stag,
        to tourists meet, and meat to eat, they charge upon the horde;
the shout is raised, the entertainment praised,
        but I retain my frown -

- In my purple cape
        and in my purple gown,
I stand amongst the gore,
        and see - my thumbs are down!

Simon Francis

I SEE A FOOL, AND THEN I DON'T

He's just a fool
A clown in fact
He just larks around
And puts on an act

He won't have a brain
Just an empty head
By the look of him
And by what he has said

But as life goes on
And when you're in need
It is that same clown
That will do the good deed

So don't judge a book
By the look of its cover
It's the goodness inside
That stands one from another.

Bert Quennell

CRUISING THE MIDDLEWICH BRANCH

Alone at the tiller, enjoying the sun,
I passed a peculiar young man.
He lay on the towpath clad only in shorts -
I assumed he was getting a tan.

The countryside round us was empty and still
And, smiling, I passed the man by
Then entering a bridge-hole forgot about him
Till behind me I heard a faint cry.

Now steering a boat is quite tricky and so
I couldn't look back then and there,
But once through the bridge-hole I risked a quick glance
And that glance quickly changed to a stare.

The young man was standing in profile to me
And I had to look twice to make sure
For though he stood upright, quite proud and erect,
His shorts now reclined on the floor.

But the very worst part of that terrible act
Wasn't witnessing something obscene,
It was having to wait till my husband appeared
Before I could tell what I'd seen!

Robbie Burton

WHO ARE YOU?

Who are you? This person I have spent most of my life with

Who are you? The someone I thought I knew?
Who are you? no one knows (We think we do)

We spend a whole lifetime together (or nearly)
But do we ever know anyone really?

We skim the surface, we know the pieces we are allowed to see
The same I know, I allow him to see of me

What is going on? What is on your mind?
What are you thinking? This person I thought I knew
If I delve deep enough, what will I find?

Will I find as you look at me you are also thinking
Who are you?

You are I should imagine asking the same questions
Will one of us die before we discover
We know what we have been, a friend, a foe or a lover.

But who are you?

Jean Roberts

A WORKING GIRL IN CHESHIRE

Conjuring pictures of Cheshire life to me -
Brings visions of hold ups on the M63

Forget yonder fields which miles along beckon
It's traffic cones mainly of which I have to reckon.

Destination accomplished and nerves again intact,
I'm contemplating the pub and that is a fact.

Dinner time looms and the venues sorted
Let's go to the *Old Cock* I suggest before my idea's thwarted.

Having a feeling for nature and an empathy with an occasional shrub
I marvel at the fields on the way to the pub

Downing a lager for social purposes only
We leave the inn and stroll back slowly.

The office block appears and I feel a compulsion
To run away and evade a revulsion.

A free spirit must be my destiny
Not cooped up in an office or a psychotic victim of the M63.

Subconsciously I say get back in there girl and earn some cash
The weekend's almost here and you can make a dash -
To explore the county and pretend to act flash.

Deborah Medina

THE WELL AT BEESTON CASTLE

The wasted well
Once succour to beleaguered sentinels
No longer proves protection for a hoard -
Has substituted gold and silver's pretty penny
For a confetti of discarded paper wrappers.

Stone-clad cylinder of darkness,
Percolating legends from the dark
Water-table of uncharted time;
A barometer of the pressures of the past.

A buried mast
Flying the flag of the centuries' surrenders
Rooted deeply in the bedrock of amnesia.

The castle's stones cry out
In proclamation of a glorious past,
But the dark life-blood of the line
Seeps insatiably away
Back to the sandstone of the
Salted seabed of unreported time.

M H Wood

RACEFIELD

Before you were torn down to become a car park
you looked beautiful - standing in your own grounds
A swing in your yard which was never empty during
the day - little girls fought for a turn on you.
Elderberry trees stood by to keep you hidden and cool
Your chimney stacks, the grandest in the town
You wore a beautiful ivy apron like the house mother.
your halls rang with shouts of joy and laughter
then the crying of home sick children.
singing and ring games were played in your *school-rooms*
your brown lino floors shone.
your playroom held victory parties and Christmas dinner
during the war your cellars house many a frightened child.
the banisters were kept polished by girls' knickers
your big iron gates were removed to help fight a war
some of your *scholars* remember you as a beautiful old
mansion and not a car park.

Dee J Darlington

KILLING SKILLS

Mesmerising terrifying
Life resulting nil,
Police defying people crying
Drugs just once can kill.

Children sniffing
Wanting something more,
Dreamy drifting
Nightmares, falling, every nerve is sore.

Aching limbs
Eyes that stream
Ideas dim
Gone that gleam.

Destroying, killing
Children, brothers,
Sisters, all are willing,
Grieving fathers, shattered mothers.

The point of this
Well what's the point,
The needle is the point,
The glue, the pills
The powders' thrills
The end result
is one that kills,
Drugs, who needs the pain.

Carol A Bissett

DELAMERE FOREST

Oh whispering leaves among your tall trees
The flutter of sunlight between
In Winter your branches so stately and bare
In Summer how full and how green
In Springtime you herald the pleasures to come
In Autumn a sight to be seen

A thousand small creatures are there at your feet
A squirrel has made you his home
When evening time comes and the wood is still
The foxes and badgers may roam

What pleasures you give to us all in our time
The walkers and people like me
Happy to wander your dappled glades
The beauty of your world to see

Our children have happily played on your floor
The memories always remain
When they are grown at whatever age now
They return but again and again

When Christmas time comes we take you home
To dress you up with glee
A part of Delamere Forest
For everyone to see
Oh may the grandeur you provide
Be with us evermore
So generations still to come
Can walk your forest floor.

Dorothy Carline

CHILDREN IN NEED

Around the world there seems no end
Of want and hunger, grief and pain

The children of the boat people, orphaned perhaps by pirates,
End up in camps behind barbed wire, unwanted.

The street children of Rio, begging, stealing, eating scraps,
A nuisance to be eliminated, their bodies dumped like refuse.

The Eritrean children we've all seen on T V
With swollen bellies and matchstick limbs.

Eritrea, Bosnia, Mozambique, Sudan, and many more
Victims of war and drought, or, further east, the flood.

The ghetto children of the USA born into drug addiction
Many without fathers; mothers, children themselves.

Or nearer home, the mentally retarded
Whom no one wants, or likely, ever will.

How shall they develop, denied the love and care
That is their need, how can they learn?

Some battered, even babies, some abused, not understanding;
How shall they grow up straight and not deformed?

Is it a lot to ask to have enough to eat,
To share a family's love and laugh with friends?

Yes, it seems to be for millions upon millions
Whose parents are too poor for even basic needs.

Many are still sold to neo-slavery, or child prostitution.
How many baby girls are left to die?

This fraction of the evils done, must make God weep.
Is this a time for red nosed comedy? How can we laugh?

Perhaps, a laughing world may be more generous
And drunk with laughter give, and laugh and give again.

But weeping or laughing, the only word is give
Laughing give all you can, weep you can give no more.

Ernest Blewitt

THE DRUNKEN DUCKS OF NANTWICH TOWN

If you go to Nantwich Town, watch out,
At noon, the drunken ducks come out:
Of strong beer they've had their fill,
As onto Welsh Row they spill.

The traffic is stopped for miles around,
As in zig zag lines they're homeward bound;
Along the road they swagger and sway
And quack at passers-by on the way.

The motorists honk their horns in anger,
But the ducks are in a stupid languor:
The local police try in vain
To clear the ducks from the terrain.

And even the Vicar of St Mary's admonishment
Has no effect, to his astonishment.
But when butcher Welch appears with his cleaver,
They all rush off to the River Weaver.

They travel down river at a furious rate
Till they reach the safety of Nantwich Lake.
The traffic moves on, and peace is restored,
But the ducks on the lake look frightfully bored.

Philip H Dobson

JIGSAW PUZZLE

How snuggly we fit together
Lying here
Like the pieces of a jigsaw
My knee cupped in the bend of your leg
My arms encompassing your waist
My chin tilted upwards
Fits the hollow of your shoulders
So precisely
We must have been chiselled
From the same stone block

Strange to consider then
The fraying tempers
And the jagged edges
Of the waking hours
How your touch freezes me
And my very presence
Sets your nerves on edge
Strange, so very strange
And that's the puzzle really.

Anne Williams

CHESHIRE LIFE

Every day, everywhere
In Cheshire, I see
People, who love to live
In Cheshire just like me.

Cheshire full of sunshine
Cheshire full of love,
Fields, farms, animals
Sent from him above.

Cheshire is an opportunity
To see the life there is
Of industry, farming, museums of
History, shopping, canals and
Wartime memories.

In this county full of
life,
I see them every day,
People living in harmony,
Cheshire's not all grass and hay.

Terri Wiseman (13)

ANDERTON LIFT

Soaring skyward, thrusting,
dormant transport
from a bygone age.

Man-made limbs,
slumbering silently
in tangential pose,
shout soundlessly to the enthusiast
'look, I sleep'

H_2O the purveyor
dark, deep
siamese partner
in an incestial love affair.

19th Century Aquarius
waits patiently on the modern day
and waits, and waits . . .

Glenn K Murphy

GAWSWORTH MORN

I've been afraid for so long now
But somehow fear is fading.
All around is freedom
Fields, flowers, sky.
Birds are lifting up their wings
As high as they can go
England in the springtime . . .
Sun's reflection on the houses
Turning grey to pink
Buds are bursting on the branches
The pine reach the sun above.
Floating drift the clouds . . .
I don't want today to end
Is it love I've found? . . .
With
       A village
       With a sky
With daffodils all around.
It is heaven I have found?

The day began cold and dark
Yet promise was around
With brightest yellow
Deepest pink
Covering the ground.

Ingrid Friedmann

CHESHIRE SAM

'Cheshire Sam' has travelled far and wide,
Building bridges and stemming tides;
Constructed Europe's vast motorways,
The M25 with friends he laid.

'Cheshire Sam' is now back home,
His body ravaged no more to roam;
By the Weaver he does dwell,
Colourful tales he has to tell.

'Cheshire Sam' looks out, Anderton Lift he views,
Meeting Boatmen and exchanging news;
Observing Cheshire's mammoth Victorian structure,
British Waterways 'wonder', my. . . what a picture.

'Cheshire Sam's' life is coming to an end,
His joints are still and he cannot bend;
'Lifts' heritage assured, Sam raises a cheer,
His work is over, friends hold him so dear.

Fay Mandeville

CHESTER CROSS, SATURDAY AFTERNOON (ABOUT HALF PAST ONE)

Buy one, get one free,
Last day of the Sale,
You can give to Cancer Research,
Or you can save the Whale.

Live-a-little Sir,
Buy the girl a ring
Finest costume jewellery
Plastic's the in-thing.

Hear the buskers play Presley
While Coco mimes to the stars
Not enough money to go 'round
And too many flamin' guitars.

David J Glover

OUR VILLAGE

Where in the world would you find
A prettier spot than ours?
Coaching Inn, school, trees, farms,
And fragrant wayside flowers.

Davenham has much history,
In the Domesday Book, you know,
Has clear and steepled skyline,
And wild birds come and go.

Between the Weaver and the Dane
We played and worked in fields,
Held picnics, reaped golden corn,
As three sheaves upon shields.

Lovely folks in days gone by,
Graced our village scene,
With courtesy and helpfulness,
Shared meals when times were lean.

Proud sons left this hamlet,
To answer twice the call,
Laid down their lives for Davenham
For our homeland they walked tall.

I've loved my Cheshire village
Since nineteen thirty-five
As sweet as the honey bee
Homing to its hive.

This is my delightful village
That has truly been my home.
To here I have returned
From days spent on the roam.

Through our pleasant dwelling
The traffic rumbles past,
Not for much longer
A by-pass is planned - At last!

J Conboy

THE CHESHIRE CAT

There's a cat that lives in Cheshire
he grins from ear to ear,
But if you try to catch him
he can simply disappear.

His name is known in many tongues
Of which there are quite a few,
In the tongue of utter nonsense
It's Diddle-di Diddle-dum Do.

While her sister was reading
Alice fell asleep,
The Cheshire cat entered her dream
Just to have a peep.

He once went to America
He went with Royal Mail,
he hid under Davy Crocket's hat
And all you could see was his tail.

When Royalty visit Cheshire
And on occasions they do,
The cat greets them with a smile
Saying 'Howdy Doody Do'.

So when you visit Cheshire
Look underneath your hat,
And you may, if you're quick enough
See the Grinning Cheshire Cat.

C Dennison

CHESHIRE

Cheshire - the deformed perversion of capitalism,
Where the rich live in their incorruptible paradise,
Blind to all the sufferings of the world,
All except their falling house prices.
 Whose beauty has been disfigured with acid greed,
The unnatural fields of submissive, drugged grass - crucified with wire
 and stakes,
Unresponsive and alien animals in a tamed, trained sea, tainted with
 green blood

By the rapers by the forest.
The strangled asphyxiated screams
Of birds in the air,
begging us to leave them be;
While on the ground,
The laboured rasping sobs
Of a fox
Made lame, caught in an oblivion past exhaustion,
Before it is ripped apart,
With laughter in its ears,
Mad fear in its heart - a curse on its lips.
 Now, in a concrete jungle you live in asphalt territory,
Overshadowed by stone trees,
Not thinking, not feeling, just growing and sucking the earth dry,
Breathing out hatred and fear,
Infested with the lonely and despairing.
 Overhead black clouds gather,
Ready to spit out the poisons from our factories - revenging the torture
 and humiliation of the sky,
While we hide from the present in houses where we too can find oblivion,
Laughing with others who have refused to be tied down.
We're hanging on by our finger-tips to a dream corrupted by power
 and jealousy,
Strapped on a road train to insanity, brakes eroded by greed and hate.
 Cheshire - the new Jerusalem.

David Yates

AUTUMN IN ESSEX

Grown
through green to gold.
Grain
soon to be garnered
acres the eye
across the plain
of Essex.
Here and there
a crimson field
where poppies blaze
plundering the yield.
A narrow road
teases and twines,
as, distantly a spire
spears
the sky.
Eternity!
Harvest time tears
from the year's
calendar the ripened sheaf.
The plough follows
and furrows.
The brown earth
waits,
while lying beneath
a hoary counterpane
another birth gestates.

Hilda A Bankes

THE COUNTRY OF CHESHIRE

Cheshire - famous for cheese and grinning cat,
No-one's quite sure what it's grinning at.
Farmland and pasture show calm rural life,
Belying its history of past borderland strife,
For Norman and Celt, and blonde, blue-eyed Dane
Came to slaughter and pillage, again and again.

A primeval swamp was left, when the last Ice Age melted, of salt,
                                        water and sand,
It was from this, historians say, that we all sprang,
Or our far distant ancestors crawled to the land.
The swamp, when it dried out, left salt deep 'neath the plain,
From Roman to now man has dug it again.
And although our salt-mines fill no-one with fear here,
They're the largest, they say, outside of Siberia.
We value it most for its distinctive flavour,
Add a pinch to a meal and you get the full savour.
The Romans, it is said, in those great days of old,
Prized it so much that they used it like gold.
It was prized by them most for its flavour, not calorie,
They paid soldiers in salt money, from which we get salary.
It cannot but fill the mind then with 'wundiment'.
From Centurion's salary to our table condiment.

But battles were fought on Cheshire's hills and moors,
Some helped to shape history, or turned the tide of wars.
Also reminders macabre from times long gone,
We've a Headless Woman, and a Horned one.
Cities laid siege to; and great houses burned,
There's much here to study and much to be learned.
There's more could be written of times present and gone,
But I think that's enough to be going on.

Michael Gibson

ON THE LAST DAY OF JUNE. . .

We set of in brilliant sunshine to explore,
and learn of Cheshire nature more.
In a quiet tree-lined lane,
verges Rosebay Willow-herb aflame,
we found a yellow Ladybird, with spots nix,
newly-emerged; Also a Burnet, with spots six,
dangerously dressed, in emerald and scarlet bright,
feeding on trefoil and vetch, its sources of cyanide.

Under welcome shade of splendid wood
in the Duke of Westminster's neighbourhood.
In dry leaf litter, rustling, played
young Grey Squirrels, plume-tailed,
while a sunbathe-stupored Blackbird sat asleep,
with half-eaten snail still stuck to its beak,
upon the lawn, by Hogweed, six feet high,
umbrellas white-laced against clear blue sky.

Out into the sun once more, carotene Umbellifers,
covered in red-brown Soldier Beetle carnivores,
falsely accused for their own red body fluids,
they live in harmony with 7-spot Ladybirds,
which we observed drinking Cuckoo Spit,
(or eating the Froghopper nymphs inside it?),
while above it all, Large Whites,
were frolicking in courtship flights.

We walked into fair Eccleston,
a village built on living stone,
ancient desert dunes, the rounded grains explain:
Triassic sandstone, of *Cheirotherium* fame!
Down to the broad brown waters of the River Dee,
where flashing now metallic blue, now emerald green,
A Banded Damselfly danced over Water Lilies yellow.
Then thirst drove us back, over the Earl's Eye meadow.

Christina Nienaber-Roberts

FAREWELL TO SAM

Oh Sam! Why did you have to go?
The house is so strange without you.
No eager bark, and wagging tail,
Or outstretched paw to greet me.

The carpets clean without your hairs,
The windows clear from smudges
The floor now free from muddy paws,
The door unscathed by scratches.

My knitting on the needles stays.
My book I read in peace.
But what I'd give for that eager paw,
That interrupted me.

No more do walks have the same appeal,
Now you're not here to share them.
Empty too is the back of the church,
Without your quiet presence,

No one sitting by my side;
No silky ears to fondle,
No head to stroke, no shining eyes,
No wonder I'm lost without you.

Joyce Monks

LAKELAND

The sea laps against the shore
The children bound, more, more, more.
The lakes lap against the bank,
Mountains, dank, dank.

Hills and craggs, tarns and streams
This is reality - it's not in your dreams.
Wordsworth wrote his words so true,
All about this heady brew.

68

A brew of halcyon days
An unsolved maze.
Come walking in the Lakes
It's all there, for he who takes.

Come see the sea,
The Hills, the vales.
But don't forget
About the Gales!

Dorothy A Cannon

HANDBRIDGE

The old Dee Bridge stands solid
Against the march of time
The narrow path across her leads
To a village proud and fine

In days gone by there stood a mill
Its great wheel creaked around
As water rushed beneath the bridge
It echo'd back a mournful sound

In the cold harsh grey of dawn
Like thunder in the distant sky
The incessant noise of wooden clogs
Was heard as workers hurried by

Loud voices of the fishermen
Came floating down the Dee
They took the bad times with the good
And kept their jollity

When many gathered in the pub
To drink a well earned jar
Those wooden clogs and muddy boots
Would line the Ship Inn bar

Elizabeth Hughes

REMEMBRANCE

We remember our dead from two world wars,
Having given their all in the Allied cause.
With pride on November eleventh every year
We recall fathers, sons and relatives dear,
Unselfishly making that sacrifice supreme,
So that personal freedom was not just a dream.
One particular anniversary comes to mind
Our brownie daughter joining others of her kind,
Damp cold and gusty winds preceded a storm
The big crowd shivered as the ranks began to form.
The procession for the cenotaph was about to leave,
A man with wheelchair through the mass did weave,
Pushing along his own pride and joy,
A handicapped, invalid eight year old boy.
Attired in cub uniform pressed and neat,
Regardless of weakness still up to the feat.
Around the neighbourhood the lad was well known,
With arms and legs thinned right down to the bone.
Muscular Dystrophy meant his muscles did waste,
He would never walk, let alone run in haste,
A fact not known to many a friend
Was soon, inevitably, his life would end.
He insisted to his Dad his coat remove,
To be one of the lads he had to prove.
The crowd respected the fallen of bravery raw,
But in father and son they saw even more
Raw courage and love as he took his son's coat,
Everyone to a man had a lump in their throat.
Now whenever we celebrate Remembrance Day
And the words 'lest we forget' they say,
I remember that lad of hapless plight
Who wanted to belong with all his might,
Now in the land of heroes untold
One of those who will never grow old.

C E Rushton

IT'S JUST BABY BLUES

When I had you they cut up my tummy
Because you were getting tired
Then suddenly I was your mummy
You must have wished you had died
Every morning I wouldn't get out of bed
Your daddy would shout in despair
I would drop you angrily into your cot
Then turn and leave you there
I screamed. I shouted and then cried with guilt
Because I truly loved you inside
And despite the way you were treated
It wasn't often you cried
Your little face as I slapped your leg
All crumpled and pouring with tears
Is still engraved in my memory
And will haunt me for many more years
Although you are four and I'm better now
I will never forget what I did
I look at you now and I hate myself
You are such an affectionate kid
I can't remember a lot of it now
I was robbed of our first year together
But Michael, despite how I treated you
I loved you, and will do forever
We have good days and bad days like most do
But at least now I'm here for you
I desperately wish I could turn back the clock
But there isn't a thing I can do
Please believe me that I really love you
without you my life would be lame
I am proud to say you are mine, son
I only wish you could say the same.

Dawn Riccio

THE TRAVELLER

Tales are told on Cheshire plains of battles lost and won.
Of magic and magicians and a Counties saving son.
When hope seemed lost for a travelling man
in Alderley woods alone,
he came across a holy place,
a cavern made of stone.
Sell me your horse a voice called out
for no-one else will buy.
All day at the market place no matter how he tried,
he could not sell his trusty mount,
how clear it was to see.
The spell is cast as was foretold,
not one bid was received.
So homeward bound he made his way
along the path that night,
and chanced upon the Spirit man
bathed in clear white light.
Good Sir, he said, sell me your horse
for a need greater than yours.
He led him to a secret place before great stone hewn doors,
They entered in by Pan pipes, that elvin figures play,
A chamber full of sleeping Knights,
white horses where they lay.
Except for one, so incomplete this sleeping force remained.
He turned to the Magician who smiled and then explained,
You are blessed, dear travelling man, there is no need to fear,
My quest to find the missing horse, is why I brought you here.
In years to come, when all seems lost,
this country torn asunder,
The call for help will herald forth
to Knights who lie in slumber.
This army will awake to make our England 'great' again,
as they ride out to battle upon the Cheshire plain.
The traveller marvelled at this tale, as he began to tire,
What a story this will make around a great log fire.

When he awoke from troubled sleep,
the Sage had disappeared,
together with the wondrous sights that he had so revered.
And ever since that fateful day, though many men have tried,
the Magician and his soldiers have avoided prying eyes.
This truth is now a legend that in Alderley woods remain,
perched high upon an outcrop,
above the Cheshire plain.

S Farr

AFRAID OF THE DARK

The thunder booms through the sky at night,
Alone in your room, hold your covers tight.
Don't listen to the fear inside your head,
Forget the storm. . . go back to bed.
Tomorrow you'll be safe and sound,
But as for now, better snuggle down.
Don't look in that shadow, or wonder what's there
But don't turn your back. . . I wouldn't dare!
For in your room are the ghosts of the night,
Who hide in the darkness out of your sight.
And if you hear them singing, try and stay calm,
They're only lonely, they mean you no harm.
You're alone too, and the night's getting late,
But voices in your head, they keep you awake.
'Afraid of the dark? Afraid of ghosts?
Afraid of your dreams?' That scares you the most.
So when you can't sleep, and the thunder booms,
Don't fear what's hidden in the dark of your rooms,
There's just you and your dreams, and the ghosts of the night. . .
                    . . . And if you're afraid of the dark,
                        Better snuggle up tight!

Kelly Jones

UNTITLED

Strolling through the 'Park' one day,
When passing the 'Dee' - on the way,
All was quiet - not a sound.
Only the 'Birds' - flying up and down,
And the 'Swans' - drifting along -
looking so proud,
Feeling so peaceful there -
I uttered a 'Prayer' -
'Heaven' - seemed everywhere,
How happy - all the 'World' would be,
If it was like that little corner - by the 'Dee'

F A Hudson

THE OLD MAN

He wasn't there again outside the farm:
tractors idle, yard empty, low front door closed,
pansies nodding gently in the tubs.
Over there stretched Woodford Runway and behind
the long back of Alderley Edge:
my path wound up to the Park -
but I slowed:
How was the old man I had seen several times
limping unevenly before the house?
One day his two legs were accompanied by four more -
a walking frame supported his uneasy steps.
Another time with stick he paused to greet me:
'You're early today! Much better walking; not like those idiots on the run.'
He had remembered me! And now
I was agitated: he was not there
even on my return.
I had just heard the first cuckoo of the summer -
a mocking cry across the trees
that repeated itself harshly. . .

Liz Owen

COVERING THE WATER

Silent mist comes creeping
Covering the water
Suffocating blanket
Across the pretty Dee

Black bridge of shadows
Covering the water
Stands skeletal
Suspending, encasing me in its form

Blue black sky grows overhead
Covering the water
Reflecting stars, like
Splintered jewels in tar

Ashen moon she draws me
Covering the water
Dragging, glass-like
Mirroring the depths

Light and dark fall dancing
Covering the water
Beams of life and death
Flirting before war

Outstretched hands of blackness
Covering the water
Beg for blessings
With Oaken fingers

Tears ripple on its surface
Covering the water
I add something of my own
Stillness silences my weeping

And night falls on the Dee
Covering the water.

Rachel Sprason

WALKING THE TOW-PATH

Odalisque like, winter leaning trees:
page three naked, and promising;
in dark relief, against undulating green banks
split, by a serpentine brook. . .

Gulls: Poised; Sculptural;
upon fence posts. . .
The off-season canal also still,
chill,
reflecting clouds. . .

Then, around the reeded bend,
a motor:
and avian sculpture lifts,
skybound white squalls, over water. . .

The canal too is moving:
its legs
torn apart,
effortlessly,
as the boat courses on.

Its Master looks upon me:
his gaze
abuses
the stream of my thoughts. . .

He smiles; I too:
but my thoughts,
like the water,
shall not flow
the same way
again.

Christina James-Gardiner

SEMPER SURSUM, BARROW

Semper sursum, Barrow, producing submarines,
even though the workforce is massively reduced;
still serving the Navy and also the Marines,
it's the raison d'etre that subs are being produced.

Semper sursum, Barrow, the motto of our town,
we're always uplifted by your architecture;
the industrial wheels have begun to slow down,
some products, our country no more manufactures.

Semper sursum, Barrow, looking to the future,
but no-one ever know what tomorrow may bring;
we may return to nature and agriculture,
if the pendulum completes its circular swing.

Semper sursum, Barrow, tomorrow's another day,
do not fear nuclear power or radiation;
on atomic power, it suffices to say,
equivocation is a repudiation.

Semper sursum, Barrow, nears the millennium,
constantly purchasing products from the Far East;
cars, hi-fi's, videos; what a compendium,
as our big shots with gambling chips, good feast.

Semper sursum, Barrow, we're still out on a limb,
still dreaming of bridges to Millom and Heysham;
chances of fruition may be extremely slim,
it depends upon the future planner's programme.

Semper sursum, Barrow, near the end of my rhyme,
as ubiquitous supermarkets and chain stores
keep sprouting up in abundance, all of the time,
one thing remains the same, the rain will always pour.

Louis Brophy

THE FELLS

In majestic grandeur they do rise,
Their Snow Peaked tops do face the skies,
The sun in all its Glory Shines,
To implant the sight upon my mind.

Rolling Fells and Valleys Too,
Given by God for man to view,
Ne're was there a grander sight,
To view those fells in springtime light.

Reaching to a distance far,
Nothing can their beauty mar,
Lights and Shades of every kind,
Blend to make them so refined.

With backcloth of skies so blue,
Fleecy clouds enhance the view,
Standing still I quietly muse,
Thanking God for Heavenly Views.

What hide you oh mystic Fell,
Sparkling Stream, Shimmering Lake and myriad of bluebell,

Arise my soul, sing and tell,
The Glories of the Cumbria Fell.

D Messenger

CUMBRIA

Foxgloves feed the bees in Autumn,
Gorse grabs greedily at slate,
Butterflies chase swift and swallow
O'er the hills and field and gate.

Harsh west winds screech on in winter,
Tearing at the plants and trees,
Making way for the cold Winter
Where everything, then dies and sleeps.

Springtime sees the new awakening,
Snowdrops sense it's time to stir,
Crocus crack the crumbling hedgerow,
Crisp and bright they greet the air.

Daffodils now wave and quiver,
Bringing hope to humankind,
Of the gentler warmer weather,
Where soft sunshine they will find.

Now the Summer warmth brings freedom,
Now the fields and woods can smile,
To see the vegetation flourish
And from the harshness rest awhile.

Denise Bodley

DREAMING

The house was asleep and silent,
And the old man by the fire,
Sat hunched up in the corner,
Dreaming of old desires,
His dog just lay beside him,
Hunting in dreams long gone
Of how they'd been together,
All that they had done.
Thro' the heather and o'er the hills
When both were young and strong
Startling a lark to fly up and rise,
And burst into joyous song,
When the air was fresh and clean
And the Sky forever blue.
For even in dreams of yesterday
Nothing could part these two.

Isabella Wignall

CUMBRIA

When Spring treads softly o'er the fells
And young lambs are a'leaping,
And young men's eyes begin to rove
With maidens left a'weeping.

When budding trees surround the lakes,
The thwaites, the meres, the waters,
The mothers scorn the hot young men
A'wary for their daughters.

The precious light of Summer
Brings life to leaf and stream,
The swallow high in clear blue sky
The silver trout a'gleam.

From beach to peak the tourists play
And marvel at the splendour
Of fruits and seeds all fat and ripe
And fir trees tall and slender.

When breath of Autumn chills the air
And mist rolls through the dells,
And weather changes rapidly,
There's danger on the fells.

But in the valley softer gleams
Of bracken warm and mellow,
And fellside trees adorn themselves
In russet, gold and yellow.

When Winter heaves her icy blast
And frost grips hard and bleak,
Frozen islands fill the lake
And snowcaps crown the peak.

To walker cold and weary
And sick and tired of danger,
The village inn gives warmth and food
And welcome to the stranger.

Janet Goddard

EARTHBOUND ON THE A66

Ephemera, hazy as morning mist around the base
We twinkle while the mountains grow
Mature and in their own good time
Calibrate the Universe as our
Puny, fleeting presence never will.

Extravagant beauty, flooding every sense
And threatening to petrify
The tenuous thread that sometimes tugs my soul
To transcendental leap
At sight of humbler forms.

Familiarity, age or Death
(The spider in the corner calmly spinning)
Have dulled the edge of ecstasy and left
A cloying after-taste bereft of wonder
Leaden in its Mortality.

Now evening gold, now angry indigo
Now snow capped against brittle blue
Nature's statuary cannot spark in me
The thrill, hair-raising shiver that salutes
The Infinite so fleetingly revealed
By chord of music, crafted word or bottomless sky.

This much too perfect vision does not now
Release my spirit to soar
And I must sit here, Earthbound on the A66
Musing on what I have lost and why.

Ann Chambers

NO BETTER PLACE

Have no regrets if you have never been
To lovely places you have never seen
Think of the treasures close to hand
In our beautiful Land.

The streams of people who go abroad
Travelling by air and sea and road
Seem to forget what they leave behind
Seeking joys they hope to find.
But for those who stay at home
Are countless treasures that can atone.

So what better things can there be
Than the gentle lapping of the sea
The quiet murmur of the brook
Gives way to the croaking of the Rook.

The seabird cries as it wheels overhead
or the noise of chickens being fed
So do not feel a little sad
It makes up for things we never had.

We look around and realise
The pleasures from this land arise
The beauty of the flower and trees
Are there for everyone to see.

William Banks

OPPOSITES ATTRACT

Powerful forges and bubbling springs,
Narrow winding lanes and mighty mountain passes,
Bustling market towns with traders shouting their wares,
And challenging fells where walkers retreat.

Sun and rain and rolling clouds,
Sandy pebbled beaches and lush green woods,
Dry stone walled fields are home to Herdwick sheep,
Curious cottages and grand hotels.

Heavy industry and country crafts,
Submarines and Kendal mint cake,
Changing landscapes, people, weather and labour,
Live side by side in Cumbrian life.

H Carling

THANK YOU FOR TRAVELLING REGIONAL RAILWAYS NORTHWEST

It was just before dark
When we crept up to the harbour
Its walls clasping the boats
Like a crab

The train tiptoed
Between the greasy waves and cliff face
As if the slightest jolt
Would crumble it

Like a chalk on a blackboard:
A sentence captured
In a violent flourish
Before the idea gets away

Home.
The touch of the platform unfamiliar
The open arms not pointing my way
The cold wind against my face.

Grainne Slavin

WHISPERS

The sand and shingle on the beach
Whisper of times long gone.
When chattering crowds drowned the seagulls' screech
And contented folk were as one,
Far away places beckon now
But Walney Isle stays
Unchanged, except for memories of our ancestors
Happy days.
The Tides of Walney ebb and flow
Over beaches on a par with the rest
Waves and sprays put on a show
For the few, who care to see nature at its best.

V Robinson

MY COUNTRY

England, oh England, how I love thee
Surrounded on all sides by sea
Small and compact
We grumble and moan it is a fact.

Woodlands and leafy trees
Flowers that attract the bees
Crocus and bluebells are due
Bringing a lovely carpet of blue.

I have travelled far and wide
With my loved one by my side
But no country can compare
To England, oh England, I do care.

Liza Leece

MARCHON CHIMNEY IN THE SNOW

The snow comes oft to Cumbria on the Fells,
But Mirehouse, Whitehaven, only now and then.

One 'then' or was it one 'now'?

It fell, fell deep, and slept,
slept softly upon sheets of ice.
Traffic lights green,
suspended like Cheshire cats' eyes,
crystal clear in a haze of white gauze,
saying 'go!'
when snow saying 'no!'
tankers, lined up before a slope they could not climb

Sheep so white on green grass,
so dirty grey on snow.
Black dog wagging tail,
more black than ever
held back by leash firm fixed to collar and to hand,
No harm intending, only playful chase.

Trees and bushes stand unswaying
Cold crazy foam clinging to them, unmoved

At a distance, on yonder horizon,
Marchon Chimney stands,
belching white clouds
into the early morning snow glow,
competing for majesty -
and failing.

A B Mossta

WETHERLAM - LONG AWAITED RETURN

Long awaited return -
ascending from the lowland realms
of shops and dwelling places,
rushing hordes and busy streets -
where life whirrs round like an endless belt -
of routines and rhythms, clockwork and monotony;
come hither -
a faint whisper from a bright realmed domain
of illuminated thought and inspiration
a fleeting glimpse, yet a majesty of tone,
a rarefied impression
dwelling just out of mind-sight,
yet giving sight enough to beckon me on -
I follow this rich veined realm
and come to places out of common reach,
uncommon zones,
where mind moves
and grasses sway,
and water tumbles over rocks,
a marvellous wall of high faced sloping rock
where once a year she displays
a show of snowy shapes,
etched out in criss-cross patterns.
A place to which I often return,
a place I call 'home' !

Heather Rollinson

UNTITLED

Do you wish, that you were like me,
To live amongst, nature's rare beauty.
Someone once wrote, 'I wandered lonely as a cloud',
If he were here today, he'd scream and shout aloud,
What have you done to this, our glorious land,
Electric pylons, poles, and advertising stands,
The price you pay for all of this beautiful scenery.
Whether natural, solar, wind or nuclear energy.
Are giant windmills, or even a few great cooling stacks,
We are told, it's perfectly safe, providing there's no leaks or cracks,
'cos they know best, and they know what they are doing,
The populous, they know, who's doing the foolin'
Let's not forget, the much favoured peace movement,
I wish they'd do us all a favour, and lobby their statement,
The mess they leave behind, rubbish and debris,
Declining of showers, requisites, a favour to the fleas,
Friends of the earth, I don't believe it never, ever,
Who pays for extra security and cleaning? Greenpeace? Never!
Cumbria does not have to break all the rules for publicity,
Not like those, to name but a few, like U2, so blatantly,
Scenery we have, beyond compare, hills, walks, and lakes,
To which many a party, school, and tourist partake,
Enjoying Mother Nature at her best, in every way,
Her colours of goldens and russetts, flowers and foliage each day,
Years of history, and not the kind, that is self inflicted,
As far as the eye can see, wild life as nature intended,
Vast open spaces, means freedom for barn owls and kestrels,
Heron, buzzards, fox, deer and badgers, at home amongst the fells,
We all have the right to view and to enjoy.
To protect, and to watch over, and not to destroy.

Shirley Atkinson

ULVERSTON MARKET DAY

If you park your car in the centre, at a place known as the Gill;
You can take in the pleasures of Ulverston, browsing around at will,
There's a street market, Thursdays and Saturdays,
With interesting things on each stall,
From toys to fresh food and clothing,
There's also an Indoor Market Hall,
It does tend to get quite busy.
Cos there's also a lot of quaint shops,
I think you can get anything you'll ever need,
In a town that pulls out all stops.
There's cafes, and chippies for eating,
And pub grub you'd find hard to beat,
Whatever it is that you fancy,
You'll certainly get it to eat.
There's ginnels, and alleys to wander,
Take a look, it will do you no harm,
You never quite know what you're going to find,
Intriguing and so full of charm,
The people are so warm and friendly,
They really cheer up your day,
The smiles and the laughter of people,
Perk you up, as you go on your way.
There's sometimes a street busker playing,
To his hat, you can contribute,
On the cobbled street, you will find him,
Playing his guitar or flute.
There's a Laurel and Hardy museum,
That's sure to give you a thrill,
And a monument to Sir John Barrow,
Perched high, on the top of Hoad Hill.

Kazzie Ingram

PENINSULAR JOURNEY

Let me persuade you to take a short journey -
Leave the car at Barrow Station, board a train.
This railway hugs the coast and reveals
So much more and so much further than the road can.

Pulling out from this prosaic station
Almost at once the train runs through
The Vale of the deadly nightshade. The line
brushes the sandstone ruins of Furness Abbey.
Does not the ghostly sense of the presence of the monks
send a authentic shiver down the spine?

Next the train glides into Ulverston.
How did this quiet station justify the employment
of those eminent Victorian architects, Paley and Austen.
Was it once prosperous? Indeed, yes. Ulverston Station had its hour.
Now willow herb, ivy and dog daisies flourish on the banks
But see how gracious the station is
How beautiful the lamps are. How seemly the clock-tower.

After Kent's Bank, the train will stop at Grange.
Grange-over-Sands, caught in a time warp, the definitive Edwardian seaside
town
Laid out along the prom. Still the same flower beds, the tennis courts and
putting green.
Easy to imagine the large hatted chaperones, anxiously intriguing
To ensure their pretty charges were seen, but not touched,
Spoken for, but rarely spoken to - all so fatiguing.

Now one more station in this random picture book -
One last surprise, as running over the estuary at Arnside
To be suddenly surrounded on both sides by the sea
and, should the sun shine, be dazzled by a million dancing lights.
Here sometimes a heron will rise up, and silhouetted against a white sky
Suggest a pterodactyl ancestry.

Joyce Bywood

THE LEPRECHAUN

It was in the lush green fields of the Emerald Isles,
that I lay resting for a while,
It was there amid its calm and beauty,
I espied him by the rickety old stile.

He sat on a toadstool, a needle in hand,
Stitching a fine set of clothes,
He was unaware of my presence
As he sang, clad in green and red hose.

He was so happy and carefree,
This little Irish man,
And as he went about his work
This is the song that he sang.

'I am a little Leprechaun,
I'm as busy as a bee,
And you will be most fortunate,
To catch a glimpse of me.'

Unmoving, I sat for quite a while,
Mesmerised by his vision,
I longed to stay there for ever,
So, to leave was a hard decision.

I didn't want to scare him,
So I gently joined his song,
I averted my eyes up to the clouds,
And when I looked back, he'd gone.

Perhaps it was just Irish folklore
Playing upon my contented mind
But I'd like to think it wasn't so,
As I left my thoughts behind.

J Little

JUNIPER ON CORNEY FELL

One might, some evening of mist and autumn
Travelling the unyielding, inviolate fell
And seeing the dark silent humps a little
Withdrawn from the summit in the thin grasses' lee

Consider them as secret beasts of the night emerging
To browse dumb and primeval on the moss and dew.
Or similarly seeing them under the long
Whip of the storm, the gale north to north-west
Pity them as notably passive Herdwicks
And drive on into obliterating rain.

But in this watercolour of September
Hills of evening pale as a Cotman or Sandby,
One sees them clearly as specimens of bonsai
Shaped by the north, the wind's expertise.

Confined in a terrain of stone and morass,
The knife of the rock clean at root and taper,
They have been bred some few centuries
To the whim of the hail, the tempest's will.

One with the cumuli, drawn to the pull
Of Sirius, the flurries of April snow,
Juniper in the sweep of the peregrine's eye,
By the valley and men unmolested remain.

Truly those gardeners - craftsmen of the East
Must bow to the masters: wind, hail and frost.

Diana McLoghlen

PRIDE AND PREJUDICES

Drab grey houses back to back, pollution gushing chimney stacks,
Grim faced women, scarves on heads, scruffy kids fed jam and bread,
Cobbled streets no sign of gold, folk who die before they're old.
Loud mouthed yobs with beer bellies, would they recognise a deli?
Basic diet of chips and pies, grey cloud laden, rain soaked skies.
Millions of people with no jobs, it's their own choosing, they enjoy being yobs.
No get up and go, it got up and went,
Now all their empty days are spent on bingo, gambling, down the pub,
Spending cash that is meant for grub.
Flat caps, watch fobs, walking sticks, kids in shops nick pick'n'mix.
Turban clad wives, fag in mouth, nagging at their drunken spouse.
Backstreet dustbins, roaming dogs, lifeless workers in heavy clogs.
Redundancy, debt, empty days, what can they do to change their ways?
'Go on your bike', move down south, learn to speak with plum in mouth.
Get on a diet, go macrobiotic, get healthy, happy, busy, erotic.
You'll still be at risk from sickness and stress, smoggy air, fumes on your
chest,
They'll mock your accent, tell friends you're queer, don't fit in, belong down
here.
No peace of mind, or quality of life, all work and travel, ideal for strife.
Don't be judgemental, keep your mind free, listen and learn, believe what you
see.
Good health, love, peace and laughter, these are the things that truly matter.

Linda Cannings

THE FALCON

Swooping through the ages
On feathers of wood and plaster
Wrapped tightly around
The breast of convivial cheer

The ale house coos and caws
Amidst the clink of bulbous glass
The splash of foaming beer

Perched on Royal soil
It sits and flies in all times
As bright quick eyes dart
From leaded panes

Waiting
Inside and out
For Cromwell's men
And the ghosts not yet born.

John Eccles

THE BEAUTY OF BARROW

How can I say in so few words
What Barrow means to me,
This sleepy, little peaceful town
Washed gently by the sea,
Where cattle graze in grass of green,
And birds sing way up high,
Where mountain hilltops, clad in snow
Laze back against the sky,
Where country lanes edge bluebell fields,
And streams and rivers flow,
Where sun goes down on shimmering seas,
And blustery breezes blow,
Where people greet you with a smile,
And pass the time of day,
You ask what Barrow means to me,
Much more than words can say.

C Molloy

TO THE LAKES AND BACK

Driving my car I leave the inner city greyness behind,
along with its tower blocks, busy streets which hustle with impatience.
I arrive via motorway with its hypnotic drone and
three lane straightness,
I am glad to leave it.
The lanes narrow, twisting its spaghetti like lines, up, down,
through, over and between the green.
This is Cumbria with its Lakeland stone,
and craggy rocks that litter the hillsides,
along with heat mist that covers its tops.
Down by the Lakeside ducks nestle the shingle,
while swans glide on water with elegance and grace.
I feel free here, I enjoy its space,
its solitude and serenity.
There could not be two more opposite worlds
whose only connection is one straight road,
but travel it back I must,
to my inner city for what it is worth, with
its pollution, noise, litter, and grey.
One day I'll come back I promise myself,
one day,
one day,
one day.

Brenda Pritchard

BUTTERMERE

Beautiful, cool and crystal clear
Lies the lake of Buttermere.

How sweet to walk its pebbled rim
In twilight's hush, when shadows dim,
Now winter's storm no longer raves
Hiding the churchyard's quiet graves.

94

All is soundless, all is still
Save for the water's gentle lap
And in the depth of Burtness Wood
The imperceptible rise of sap.

Above the crags and dew-kissed glade,
Where flowers nestle in the shade,
Buzzards soar in effortless flight
Before my eyes. . . a joyous sight.

Dusk settles with the lowering sun
And now my stroll is almost done.

The evening sunlight tints the clouds and
Cloistered peace enfolds the land;
Whilst darkening hills and fells surround
The lake . . . with a silence so profound.

Patricia S Winder

UNTITLED

For every death on this planet,
A new life is registered,
Every second of every day,
A baby is born,
And an old man dies,
Grief and death,
Are things we all must face,
Experience makes it no easier.
We can only hope for the love
Of those who care,
And ask,
Why?

Wayne Singleton

CUMBRIA

That corner of England, the most restful of all,
Wordsworth and Tourists rub shoulders
On its beautiful shores.
The Lake District hills with their grandeur and space
Give this whole dimension a feeling of grace.
The grey stone walls encompassing sheep,
The villages and hamlets for ever asleep.
The farms tucked away in the verdant green
Are just today as they've always been
The much trodden footpaths, the tourists, the cars,
All have come to admire this beauty of ours.
Ours is to conserve it, yes! but also to share
With those who can only sometimes breathe our Cumbrian air.
They have rights to tread footpaths, see sunsets and lakes.
But all of our children who we'll never meet
In generations to come, when we are asleep,
Must also see Cumbria, just as today,
The magic, the majesty, we can't take away.

Linda Fleming

CUMBRIAN RIDDLE

Ringstone round,
sentry on the fell,
solitary sentinel,
tell me -
do the mountains breathe,
do the valleys sleep
beside the dark, still waters
where ghosts of legends creep?
Do the rolling, white waves break
in time to sea-birds' screams?
What is this vast, uneasy peace
you send into my dreams?

Shelly Tomlinson

A HOME-COMING

Awake, in Ramsden's shattered dream
I walk, a mile or two from sleepy bed
Through windy streets, with aching feet
And pass the old men
On their benches, industriously bred
Staring starkly at the brick red walls
That bound the intersection of each grid.
Weeds press up through the stone
The only patch of green.
Though there's the con trick, quietly said
Of some trees at the railway stop
Or running along the old road
Into this industrial retrograde
Amongst the tourist trap
Of ghylls and becks and hills and trecks
And green fells mirrored in the lakes.
The lyric here is more disjointed
Disturbed by echoes, clangs and shouts
From ghostly rivetteers
Or the hooting of some long-gone vessel
Still resonating in our fears
Of unemployment
                    dying trade
A town to breed the renegade.

And yet it's coming home to me
A Home-Coming it seems to be
Though born amongst the border hills
I watched them closing down the mills
And witnessed as a solemn child
Tough industry becoming mild.

Robert Douglas Derbyshire

ODE TO GRANGE

It seems so very long ago
I came to live in Grange,
For years I loved the city life
I found it really strange.
All the people seemed so old,
No young ones could I see,
Perhaps they hid when I went by
Or were they having tea?
Each day I walked along the prom
To catch the train at eight,
At night when I returned to Grange
Perhaps I was too late!
As time went on I settled in,
Some friends I found at last,
Maybe life will not be bad
Now twenty years have passed.
My husband, children, all live here
The place I found so strange
No other place in all the world,
Would I exchange for Grange.

Sheila (Grange) Tyson

CONISTON WATER

Grey flurries darken the water,
sails flap and fill,
ropes pull on tightening hands.
Bodies held in taut inertia
intuitively balance
the boat's leaning bulk.

Sails dip
as the wind changes
and then are driven
by unexpected gusts;
skimming effortlessly
over cresting waves.

Irene Hrynkow

OLD TOWN - NEW TOWN

As a little child I often wandered down leafy lane amidst fields of corn,
Or along a towpath that meandered, under bridges and past a barn.
You say how idyllic was this place, can you tell me what is its name?
Perhaps I might gaze upon its face, and your childhood haunts reclaim.

I remember that at Halton Brook, my sister and I for shrimps would fish,
Not with line and baited hook, but with cupped hands to make a dish.
On a summer day when work was over, mother would take our bucket and
                                                                spade,
To Ferry Hut down by the old transporter, to build sandcastles and to wade.

Sometimes we would watch the farmer, cut the golden waving corn,
With his dusty, bright red harvester, until the fields were bare and shorn.
We would walk along the rabbit track, and visit the Castle on its mount,
To look for a cross on a donkey's back, or play on a cartwheel roundabout.

Yes, this place was Runcorn town, before the New Town planners came,
With their bulldozers to tear it down, and make Old Runcorn just a name.
Where once stood woods and pastures, grey concrete houses have been built,
Gone the freedom and the laughter, gone the ghost in Byron street.

But surely these memories all are ancient, your recollections faded and old,
Since Runcorn was so small and pleasant, lying among fields of gold!
No I am not grey and old, but my memories all have vanished,
Now only concrete grey and cold, my childhood world has banished.

Eileen Wiggins

A JOYFUL POEM

I've lived around here all my life -
Didn't want to move away.
It was in Lancashire but then
'Twas Cumbria next day!
As a paramedic I drive round
The valleys and the hills,
There's nowhere better I could work.
It's Paradise on wheels.
The changing seasons come around
And alter all the views -
It's like new starts as through the year
It changes scenes and hues.
The evergreens are joined in spring
With flowers as they bloom,
But those all fade as others come,
And die to give them room.
The summer's full of 'Joie de vivre'
With nature in full swing,
Making sure that all the flowers
Have the best of everything.
'Till Autumn comes and colours change
To Yellows, golds and browns,
The summer flowers fade away
As the year moves around,
The winter snows they cover all
Like Christmas cards to see,
Till Springtime starts it all again -
It's such a joy to me.

C Wilding

THIS LAKE DISTRICT

Oh! what splendour has been thrust up
The subterranean burning ghettos,
Conspire to wreak their beauty and havoc
On the still surface.

The weathered oaks and birches
Tremble in anticipation
Before becoming engulfed in the frenzied flames
This shivering terrain
Sculptured by deep forces.

Quiet and cool now
Great boulders slumber
Through the effervescent clouds
Huge and domineering
Majestic peaks
Cosset the beckoning silent deep waters.

Tranquil aromas whisper on a mischievous breeze
The lone daffodil
Respondent and defiant, shouts out
'This, yes, this is my land'

Soft underfoot we walked in awe
This sweet grass
This reliable rock
This solitary peace
This beauty
This Lake District

Oh! what splendour has been thrust up.

J Knake

JOHN OF THE VALE

On that bleak December morn,
Audrey, me and Nell,
stood amongst those weathered stones,
standing over privileged bones
that lie on Naddle Fell.

John Richardson lies buried where
the western wall once stood,
till seeing that the graveyard's span
couldn't take another man,
they walled another rood.

A poet and a teacher, John,
he started life an artisan,
building walls about this place
where now he lies at rest with Grace,
a truly noble man.

He spent his whole life near this spot,
this vale he loved so well,
and should the scholar e'er elect
to study Cumbrian dialect,
he has many a tale to tell.

But best of all Jack's tales I think
our favourite one must be,
of when he went to court his lass
and stood there 'jiken on t'glass,
frae back o't' laylick tree'.

And as we stood there musing,
the way a dreamer does,
'Who's that?' I thought I heard him say,
and then we turned and walked away,
'Why Jack - it's nobbut us.".

Derek Robinson

COMBE TO MAN

The hills, with mountains ranged behind, revealed by first light;
A light so transparent, that transparency to the hills it lends,
Clear clarity, lucid to the point of transition.
A transition merging to reality, as risen sun, once low and weak
Climbs higher, to reveal his power in all its fullness.

In red faced majesty, he chases ephemerality, to substantiate
The rolling uplands of of gauzy wispiness
With hills all verdant green,
With specks of grey, where lambs do play.

Then rising high, great Phoebus shows the yellow,
From way up in the sky.
The yellow, once green, but plucked by man;
The mouths to feed of human clan.

Night comes with the setting of the sun: all brilliance gone.
Mountains etched like purple shapes from other climes,
Having crept into our modern times.
With hills nestling at their feet, as though in retreat,
From the encroaching night.

The purple night is stabbed with light,
As lamp lit windows lustre, to all in sight.
While his majesty from on high, has dropped down across the sky.
A ball of fire, subdued, its duty done;
Reflections leave from what was once the sun.

Reflections thus, tip purple tops, with one last shot of yellow light:
A sight which makes the heart stand still,
As hushed within the night,
The thrill of life is implanted within the will.

A Farish

NICE LITTLE TOWN

Barrow-in-Furness, considered by us to be the best
Builder of ships, submarines, that have stood the test
Sailing the seven seas, with admiration
And defending our shores from threatened invasion.

Craftsmen plying their trade with an ideal
Platers fashioning the hulls of steel
Welders joining seams, with torch and rod
Local fishermen, catching plaice and cod.

Situated on the bay, a stone's throw from the motorway
A haven of green, where historical ruins lay
Villages and farms surround the vicinity
With lakes and fells in close proximity.

Friendly people, with friendly faces
A day on the beach, or a day at the races
Local markets, and car boot sales
Pubs and clubs, stocking local ales.

Terraced houses, semi's and bungalows
New or old, together in rows
Vanishing in unison, the small corner shops
Superstores, and supermarkets, shopping non-stop.

Gas and oil rigs, drilling their field
Pumping ashore the finds that they yield
From a community, built of necessity
By an employer, who enjoyed years of prosperity.

T W Evans

FANTASY LAKELAND

Sea's blue first grey with rain,
Grass green, but hay is beige.
Drive carefully, a winding lane,
Winds are strong and express much rage.

Sun is out, yellow flowers,
Lie on hills for hours and hours;
Wordsworth inspired by this place:
Potter's grey rabbit, making lace.

Mountains blue, purple top
There's a sheep, hair like a mop,
Clear water down the falls,
Crickets in grass; purrs and calls.

One white cottage, man keeps cow,
In one sty, a pregnant sow.
White cottage in the sun.
Sits in garden, '*lunch*' home-made bun.

Lovely flowers, foxglove, heather,
Valley of green gives much pleasure;
How sweet just to be alone,
Honeysuckle, must be home.

Carla Griffiths

CUMBERLAND

Over windswept fells, and rocky shores
To places where the eagle soars
From the solitude of high hills
To bustling town with chattering tills
The home of poets, shepherds, and kings
Its past is full of all these things
No better place to live and love
To lift one's spirits to heaven above
No place on earth to match the charms
Of summer's blossom round fellside farms.

R S Woolley

BARROW-IN-FURNESS, CUMBRIA

In the park on a Sunday
It really is a fun day,
Swans swimming in and out
Ducks waddling along the ground,
Swings, slides and roundabouts
Many pleasures to be found.

Flower beds, the trees, the shrubs,
Ice cream sold in cornets or tubs
Tennis courts, and bowling greens,
A more pleasing sight couldn't be seen.

Children's laughter, the bird songs heard by many as they row along.
Pets' corner where all may visit
Watching the budgies and peacocks as they sit.

Walks galore, seats to sit upon
Beautiful greens for children to roll on,
Or for any who wish to lay
Watching the clouds drift away.
Sunday in the park, you see
Fills us all so full of glee.

P R Martindale

THE CASTLE WOOD

How we played in the castle wood
Full of mystery and strange sounds
Crows nesting in the trees above
Rustling noises on the ground

In the Spring the snowdrops grew
Then the hyacinths all dressed in blue
The Patten flowing through the wood
Made the Summer days feel good.

Blue skies smiling through the trees
Scent of roses, sound of bees
Leaves falling to the ground
How we sang and danced around

The frosts of Autumn filled the air
Glowing berries everywhere
How I wish that I could
Play again in the castle wood.

Doreen Moscrop

THE EDEN VALLEY

Everyone talks of the Lake District, and I know it's very nice
But I know where I'd send folk, if they asked for my advice
Around the Eden Valley, with its villages way up high
You can't better the panoramic views, so easy on the eye
There's Cotehill and Armathwaite, and Ainstable as well
There's Kirkoswald, Langwathby, and Lazonby Fell
When you go to all these places, fields and trees are all you see
And there are lots of other villages throughout the valley
You can see the river Eden slowly winding on its way
Sometimes hardly moving, sometimes a torrent in play
Everything is peaceful in its coat of greeny brown and blue
Especially in autumn, when the leaves are changing hue
So instead of busy highways, and throngs around a lake
Why not go through the Eden Valley, and a quiet journey make.

Marjorie Carr

EASTER DAY, CARLISLE CATHEDRAL

For six long weeks of Lenten fast the church
Was clothed in sackcloth and the altar bare.
No flowers bedecked the pulpit nor the tomb
Of Senhouse Prior nor the altar-stair.
No frontal bright with gold adorned the board
Where sacramental Eucharist is said
And penitential prayers to God outpoured.
Bur now 'tis Easter Day and ah! how changed
The church appears from cheerless days of Lent.
White lilies blazon forth their praise, and ranged
Against the choir stall's foot fair daffodils
Their gilded trumpets raise to greet the morn
When Christ Our Saviour triumphed o'er Death's chill
And burst Hell's chains to open wide the gates
Of Paradise for base and sinful man.
The blue starred vault with hymns reverberates,
Borne heavenwards on the breath of men and boys
Whose duty and delight it is to sing
His everlasting praise with joyful noise.
In mitred splendour high above the throng
The bishop kneels and prays for peace on earth,
And voices soar to God in Paschal song.
The service ended and the blessing given,
The thundering organ's loud crescendo swells,
The closing diapason echoing up to Heaven.

Margaret Mayne

ROMAN REMAINS

Just beyond the lip of the horizon.
Gentle clouds kiss peaceful hills.
Snow covered lonely fells turn bright
Silver, where the sunbeam spills.

I gaze on enduring, enchanted Skiddaw.
Contemplate changeless Carrocks mass.
From the place where the Roman soldier
Stood sentry, waiting for time to pass.

Did he also turn, like me, to the Solway.
Criffels' bulk, blue, majestic and old
And see the grey gulls go a-soaring.
Feel the raw helm wind, harsh and cold.

Watch golden corn grow in the Valley
Sheep on the abundant, life-giving Plain.
With a smile see sweet skylarks rising,
But, wish in his heart he was home again.

To his birthland of continuous sunshine.
No frost or hail on his face to sting.
Or did he love the changes of seasons,
Winter and summer, autumn and spring.

The village around him has gone now.
The fort deserted, the stones used again
But nothing can change the horizon,
Or the calm and beautiful Solway Plain.

Time can go back in our memories.
Loved ones returned to our mind's eye.
But nothing can stop time passing.
Only the bird in the cage cannot fly.

Mary Heslam

GREENACRE

In the *history of Read* by the late reverend Greatorex
We feature quite firmly,
Then being part of the rural council of Burnley.
Read Hall when built in 1342, the Lord of the Manor one never knew
Until, Sir Richard De Greenacre married John De Clough's daughter,
The De Cloughs at that time seemed to own bricks and mortar,
And so all around the peasants paid homage
Even the heron in flight then could show off its plumage!
But times were to change, here the church featured strongly
It acquired five acres, the rent paid at Whalley (2 white gloves)
Now, to bring the story up to date
These houses were built 1948
Twenty seven in all to enlarge this village
Built in council design, made a modern day spillage,
And when again from the past a name was sought
A few were thought but came to nought.
Then the reverend who wrote this past history of Read
When asked thought that Greenacres would suit,
For once, we were, the old football field,
With flora and fauna to boot!
There are two churches, a school and shops close by
All gratefully used by my husband and I.

J Ward

INFORMATION

We hope you have enjoyed reading this book - and
that you will continue to enjoy it in the coming years.

If you like reading and writing poetry drop us a line,
or give us a call, and we'll send you a free information
pack.

Anchor Books Information
1-2 Wainman Road
Woodston
Peterborough
PE2 7BU